W9-CSV-545

Of
Course
I'm
Biased

"Dr. Maclure writes with a rare blend of British understated, self-deprecating humour and wit seasoned by long experience in medicine, marriage, music and many other activities on at least three continents, and especially by a passionate and transparent Christian faith. He transforms the most trivial and the most profound events alike into a great read."

-Dr. A.J. Voth, M.D. F.R.C.P. (c)

"Dr. Maclure's life is one lived in true sacrificial service to Christ. That's what readers will find in his latest book *Of Course I'm Biased*. Written with clarity, widom and a delightfully dry British wit, it is a pleasure to read an inspiring example to every believer interested in relevant shoe-leather Christianity."

-Mark Pickup, Advocate for Disabled
and Founder of "Human Life Matters."

DR. HUGH MACLURE

OF COURSE
I'm Biased

Belleville, Ontario, Canada

Of Course I'm Biased
Copyright © 2003, Hugh L. Maclure

All Scripture quotations, unless otherwise specified, are from the
Scriptures marked NIV are from *The Holy Bible, New International Version*.
Copyright © 1973, 1978, 1984 International Bible Society. Used by permission
of Zondervan Publishing House. All rights reserved.

Scripture quotations are also from *The Holy Bible, King James Version*.
Copyright © 1977, 1984, Thomas Nelson Inc., Publishers.

National Library of Canada Cataloguing in Publication

Maclure, Hugh L.
    Of course I'm biased : writing from a Christian world view-
point / Hugh Maclure.

ISBN 1-55306-591-3

    1. Christian life. I. Title.

BV4510.3.M33 2003   248.4   C2003-902772-4

Illustrations by author.

For more information, please contact:

Hugh Maclure
311 2910 109 St.
Edmonton AB T6J 1H4
(780) 437.2844

Guardian Books is an imprint of *Essence Publishing*. For more information, contact: 20
Hanna Court, Belleville, Ontario, Canada K8P 5J2.Phone: 1-800-238-6376 • Fax: (613)
962-3055 • E-mail: publishing@essencegroup.com • Internet: www.essencegroup.com

Table of Contents

$\mathcal{F}$oreword

HUMOUR (modified Scottish type), impiety (Anglican kind), insight (attained by lifelong reflection) and understated brilliance (a natural gift disciplined by his profession and good DNA) mark Hugh Maclure's essays on "thinking Christianly." This is an accessible and penetrating look at ourselves, issues of concern in culture and the church from a loving "elder's" perspective. He shows us both our foibles and as many strengths. He loves the church and his critique comes from his love backed by a lifelong service (and it is a lifelong service; Hugh is eighty-five years old).

Such a remarkable life: British Colonial medical officer during WWII in West Africa; medical missionary in West Africa, Haiti, Uganda; general practitioner in "oil town" Alberta and lifelong servant; and small "p" prophet for the church. Hugh writes about it all.

His writing is what he defines as the "third category," which he explains as implicitly Christian, assuming the evangelical /orthodox faith rather than either declaring or defending it.

His topics range from the very humorous (Angus and his frustration with contemporary worship in Chapter 6) to the troubling and prophetic essay on civil disobedience, Chapter 12, with stories of family, medical practice and personal experience interspersed. Of special significance is his autobiographical recall of his youngest son's death from AIDS, followed by a profoundly important if somewhat polemical defense of the biblical view of the debate around the matter.

I read this book because of my affection and respect for the author. For you who don't know Hugh Maclure, you will be introduced to a truly wonderful human who, in humble, disarming fashion, lets us converse with him about the most significant issues of any time, "thinking Christianly."

Several of the essays are standouts—alone worth the purchase! My current favourite is the "ABC Problem" (Chapter 15). This succinct insight into the problem of biblical interpretation and application is Hugh at his best. I won't tell you what he does to solve the problem—go there and read it—and the rest, too.

—*Cal Netterfield, D. Min.*

Writing from a Christian World Viewpoint

YOU cannot shake off your own shadow. You cannot create a machine that makes energy. You cannot speak or write without bias. Both Christian and secular writers are biased. They either take Christian presuppositions for granted, or else ignore or deny them. An "unbiased opinion" is an oxymoron.

I try to figure out, if I can, the bias of the authors I read. Classed as "secular" would be those writers who never, ever introduce a character who is a practicing Christian, except as a caricature, even though they represent ten percent of the population on this continent. In their books, Sunday is a time for sleeping in, gardening or reading the sporting pages. The heroes of Dick Francis, for instance, in addition to being indestructible, are upright, honest, intelligent and keepers of six or seven of the Ten Commandments, but they always appear to be braving their way through a meaningless universe.

Then there are the (lapsed?) Roman Catholic writers. Their main characters still respect the priest, but are careful to let him "do" religion for them. Again, their characters are quite selective about the Ten Commandments. Tom Clancy, Graham Greene,

Frederick Forsyth and Jack Higgins are examples. All are superb storytellers, but their skill is not under discussion. Hats off to the rare exceptions, such as John Grisham, for breaking the rules and writing best-sellers with an honest look at real Christianity occasionally. Hats off, too, to the new best-selling Christian authors such as Sigmund Brouwer as they appear on the scene.

One could continue in this vein, noting the high-tech scientific materialism of Michael Crichton (but wonderfully terse and economical writing), or the disillusioned High Church Anglicanism of P.D. James; but the overwhelming impression given by the great majority of best-selling novelists is of a world on which the God of the Bible has made no impression whatever and is therefore ignored.

In reaction to this bleak scene is the growing strength of "Christian" literature. Three classes of this genre stand out. First, there are the books by Christians for Christians about Christian topics or Christian people. These include Christian novels, devotional material, autobiographies, Bible commentaries, and so on. They take up ninety-five percent of the space in Christian bookstores.

Second, there is the category of apologetics, in which philosophical, scientific or historical issues for or against the faith are discussed. I was reared on this type of literature.

Third, there is the kind of literature this book is about; i.e., writing that is implicitly Christian though not always explicitly so. Christian values and truth are quietly assumed just as implicitly as they are denied or ignored by our "secular" best-selling novelists.

Of course, many subjects are neutral as far as a world view is concerned, though even a book on mathematics assumes that truth is real, at least within the parameters of the subject!

C.S. Lewis was a shining example of a master of all three types of writing. I have read his space trilogy at least five times, and though I've never been tempted to covet my neighbour's ox or ass, this author's writing skill presents a much stronger temptation!

The following chapters are an attempt at Christian writing type three. Most of them have been published, and five of them have won awards at the Christian writers' fellowship to which I belong. This is a group that started in Alberta and is now spreading Canada-wide.

A diver's voice becomes Donald-Duck-like in quality, according to the concentrations of helium in his lungs. He cannot help it. It is a function of the atmosphere he is breathing. I believe type-three Christian writing can only arise in a similar way, when the scribe is breathing the pure unpolluted air found at the Christian world-viewpoint.

$\mathcal{H}$ockey Fright in Canada

"CHRISTOPHER'S operation successful. Recovery smooth. Four fistulae found, not one."

This cryptic telegram found its way to the hospital in Sierra Leone, West Africa, where we were working during the winter of 1987. The medical and surgical load was heavy as I was relieving two other doctors for a couple of months, so an unintelligible telegram, almost certainly mutilated in transit to this remote outpost, barely raised a query in our minds until lunch-break. We then began to ask some questions. Yes, the telegram really was for us. Yes, "Christopher" really must refer to our ten-year-old grandson. No, there were no further details.

At this point, the questions in our minds began in earnest. Fistulae? What sort could a husky young athlete develop in a few weeks? Anal? Surely not at his age. Intestinal? But he didn't have Crohn's disease, mesenteric adenitis, tuberculosis, amoebiasis and the rest. Tracheo-oesophageal? Ridiculous! Anyway, thank God the operation—what operation?—had been successful.

Since an earlier letter of explanation had gone astray, we didn't find out what happened until we got home in February 1988. (Those were pre-email days for us).

A hockey game in Edmonton, Alberta, was suddenly interrupted that day in December '87 when a young centre, noted for his speed and good stick-handling, suddenly collapsed with chest pain, breathlessness and cyanosis. He appeared to be having a heart attack. Next day at the University Hospital, it was decided that one or more potential connections in his cardiopulmonary circulation had blown open during the stress of the game. Within a week, Chris was in the OR undergoing heart surgery.

Four hours later, Christopher returned to the recovery room festooned with tubes and cables, and very much alive. After the first three pain-filled days, his convalescence was smooth. Many wonderful things happened as a result of this whole event. We are saturated with stories of horror, suffering, indignation and bitterness against God, all faithfully recorded in the news media, but the blessings and gain the Lord brings to His people through the fires of testing are often ignored. To tell some of these positive things is the purpose of this account.

1. Crises bring new opportunities for Christians to teach and learn.

The night before the operation, Chris said to his mother, "Mom, people die from this sort of surgery sometimes, don't they?" (How would *you* respond to this kind of question from your ten-year-old son?). His mother replied, "Yes, occasionally, but not often. We'd better see what the Bible has to say about the death of a believer, hadn't we?" Christopher's calmness was noted by the surgeon in his operation report.

2. Crises unite people and generate love which spreads outwards.

The sudden pressure on this family triggered an amazing response from friends and acquaintances both in and outside the church. Their pastor said he had never before seen such an out-pouring of concern. Many friends drove the 180-mile round trip to Edmonton to visit, and Chris took with him into the OR a card which had been given him with the words from Hebrews 13:5 and 6, NIV—

> *God said, "Never will I leave you; never will I forsake you."*
> *So we say with confidence, "The Lord is my helper; I will not*
> *be afraid. What can man do to me?"*

Chris' class at school sent gifts, as did his hockey team. They also sent a medal won while he was in hospital. One day during his convalescence, two enormous young men from the local Grey Cup-winning football team showed up at his bedside to inquire after "our buddy Chris."

3. Crises precipitate decisions to follow Christ.

In January, Christopher's younger sister received the Lord as her Saviour. Later, Chris and a brother were baptized. An uncle, a new Christian, said that during those weeks he had for the first time seen what real prayer and Christian love were like.

Today, fifteen years later, Christopher is a teacher in the public school system here, and his wife is also a teacher and music major from the University of Alberta. He has played in the hockey team that won the under-fifteen Edmonton city champi-onships, and was a member of a team that cycles 500 miles in seven days through the Rockies every summer. (This year we raised $40,000 for Bible Society sponsored work overseas.) He has helped build low-cost housing in Mexico. At one time he had his own gospel music band. He is now active in his church youth group, and best of all, he knows the freedom that comes from serving Christ.

Who Do You Think You Are?

Award-winning essay for Ascribe *Christian Writers' Fellowship, May, 1998.*

WHETHER one is writing about oneself as a person or as a writer, the above title fills a Scotsman's cold northern mind with foreboding. Am I to indulge in an orgy of self-revelation, letting my hopes, ideals and fantasies all hang out to be picked over by the less inhibited? Having spent a lifetime trying to think about myself less, am I to spend three pages now on concentrated introspection? Well, I suppose there's no harm in setting down my thoughts at least. After all, I don't have to submit them for publication if I change my mind.

First then, who do I think I am as person? A hard question to answer when posed by another, harder still when asked by God, and hardest of all when I ask it myself. Self-knowledge is clouded by guilt (true and false), pride, original sin and mood swings which in turn vary with one's blood sugar and electrolyte level, body temperature, hormonal activity, state of the digestion and a host of other physical, emotional and spiritual influences. Above all, there is my tendency to lapse into the Walter Mitty syndrome.

Of the many pieces of writing that can drive a would-be scribe crazy with envy (why didn't I have the wit to think of that first?), *The Private Life Of Walter Mitty* by James Thurber is high on the list in my estimation. Like me, Walter Mitty has a variety of characters he assumes when his mind is in neutral. He would find it hard to answer the question, "Who do you think you are?" While waiting for his wife in the shopping mall, he finds himself on the bridge in command of a battle cruiser steaming at flank speed, with guns blazing, into the teeth of a far superior enemy force, and emerging victorious just in time to help carry the shopping bags out to the car in the parking lot. On the way home, the family Ford transforms into a supercharged Ferrari which he drives with consummate skill, overtaking on the last curve of the Indy 500 just in time to see the checkered flag as it flashes down over the gate of 1654 Laburnam Drive. Of course, there is no end to these temporary identities.

In like manner, how many times has the mediocrity of my life (as far as human achievement is concerned), been dressed up in heroic disguise as the Walter Mitty within takes over? I confess to having occasionally imagined myself, for a few mad minutes while doing an appendectomy or hernia operation, to be a world-famous cardiovascular or neurosurgeon performing some incredible feat of hi-tech wizardry, to the admiring gasps of my amazed colleagues. Fortunately, these lapses of concentration have not, as far as I know, resulted in any damage to my long-suffering patients. Perhaps I am not alone in this kind of fancy. Are there not others who, for a city block or two, wear the Tour de France yellow jersey while cycling down to the post office, or, when jogging, frequently break the four-minute mile while puffing up the river valley hill? (Or even compose their own eulogy while attending someone else's funeral!?)

I was once asked by a surgeon in the Edmonton city hospital, while I was assisting at a hysterectomy, "Who do you think you are to go abroad and stuff your religion down the unfortunate Africans' throats?" He added quickly, "And don't give me any theology!" Before I could reply, a colleague chipped in, "Then don't ask theological questions!"

To Moses, it was a theological question alright at the burning bush, and I would have given the same sort of answer—"I am too young, I am too lazy, I am not worthy, I feel too hypocritical and incompetent to serve You in a special way." Slowly though, the lesson is sinking in as God replies, "My beloved child, what you say about yourself is all true, and it makes you uniquely qualified to be My obedient servant. I can only use those who admit their sin and weakness."

This brings us to the two great Canadian national sports: the Struggle for Identity and the Search for Self-esteem. The media pundits tell us that most Canadians spend their days in these two most unprofitable pursuits, and the few who don't should. I say "unprofitable" because that is exactly what the Lord called them (Matthew 16:24–26). Our search is to be away from self, and self-esteem, identity and fulfillment come only as side-benefits.

Bearing these cautions in mind, who do I think I am as a Christian writer? Answers to this question have developed slowly, like gray hairs and increasing girth. To begin with, I have always enjoyed writing, whether it was skits for a sing-song at camp, or articles for some magazine. Later, I began to pay more attention to style and tried to write in the crisp, economical manner of Michael Crichton, P.G. Wodehouse (said by Winston Churchill to be the finest writer in the English language!), and, of course, C.S. Lewis.

I have always had an ambition to write something with a Christian world view that would take the non-Christian world by storm; i.e., to join that select club to which C.S. Lewis, Dorothy

Dr. Hugh Maclure

L. Sayers and G.K. Chesterton belong (Walter Mitty in action again!). Perhaps as a feeble attempt to move in that direction, I decided to write an account, *Letters from the White Man's Grave*, of medical missionary experience in Africa between 1941 and 1991, and to write it as though to those friends of mine who are not yet committed to Christ and His Kingdom. This attempt has been moderately successful as far as my non-Christian friends have been concerned. This book is now in second edition and about 2,700 have been unloaded.

Other books are planned, but I can feel the lethargy of old age breathing down my neck. Meanwhile, I continue to write, and have had just enough success with magazines to feel encouraged and just enough highly flattering rejections to be 'cast down but not in despair.' Writing has also given me opportunities to speak on some technical subjects—for instance, abortion and homosexuality.

I believe God has given me a gift (though it may not be as great as I like to think!), as long as I don't spend too much time asking myself, "Who do you think you are?" I am reminded of Martin Luther's answer to the question, "What was God doing before the creation of the world?" He replied, "Preparing hell for people who ask stupid questions."

Oil Town Doctor

AT the end of November 1956, we arrived in Drayton Valley, Alberta, after the long journey across Canada by train from Montreal. The doctor I was coming to work for had sent the town ambulance to meet us at the CN station in Edmonton and bring us to our new home. After three days in the Canadian National train with three smallish boys, we needed it!

Four weeks earlier we had been perspiring in the humid thirty-seven-degree Celsius heat of Freetown, West Africa. We travelled back to England by boat while the Suez crisis brewed. The eight-day voyage was followed by two weeks of confusion as we made arrangements to emigrate to yet another continent. At last, we settled on board the *Empress of Britain* with our three boys, two of whom were quite glum to be leaving their friends and their soccer behind in England.

After a hostile encounter with a customs official (a founding member of the PQ, perhaps) in Montreal, we boarded the CN train as darkness fell. The farmland of Quebec gave way to the granite outcrops and freezing lakes of the Canadian Shield, and sheets of ice formed between the carriages as in the film *Dr.*

Zhivago, which we saw several years later. By the time the big skies and grain elevators of Alberta appeared, the boys were getting hard to entertain.

Boredom actually had not been much of a problem during the trip because of the weird behaviour of our fellow passengers. Our train seemed to have been invaded by a drunken mob of happy lunatics who sang, danced, imbibed and vandalized their way across the true north strong and free. Was this really standard behaviour for the inhabitants of our new homeland? We learned, years later, that we were in the middle of a train-load of Edmonton Eskimo supporters. Apparently, a certain Mr. Parker had scored some vital points in the last minute of the Grey Cup final against the Allouettes.

Seven days after arriving in Drayton Valley, Alberta, the temperature dropped to thirty degrees below zero (on the old scale), which was 120 degrees colder than Freetown, Sierra Leone. We did some very hurried shopping for Canadian-type winter clothes.

The initiation into oil-field life began immediately, and we started as ever in a new country by learning a new language. Words like *muskeg*, *freeze-up*, *road-ban*, *mouse hole*, *tongs*, *tool-push*, *service-rig* and *skid-shack* soon became part of our vocabulary, as well as the liberal use of such Ukrainian-Canadian adverbs as "already, then, so soon, even, again," and, of course, the sentence-ending Canadian trademark—"eh?" I remember, too, my astonishment when the first night-call came in. A young mother had just discovered, at three o'clock in the morning, that her baby had "cradle-cap." What in the world did she mean, *eh?* I had visions of an infant stuck between the bars of its playpen by its head.

We rapidly got acquainted with the town's alcoholics, starting with one who was blissfully freezing to a contented death in a snowdrift. One young man called (in the middle of the night, of course) to say he was in the process of gassing himself to death in his kitchen, and was I interested, eh? I hustled round to his skid-shack and found the oven turned on and the patient resting comfortably with his head by the wide-open window. A few weeks later, this same character stumbled through our back door and fell down the stairs into our basement—need I say, at night? We kept him there and looked after him until he was sober once more. He began to come to our weeknight Bible-study group, and years later we saw him in Vernon, British Columbia, where he was working, sober and with his act together. I wish we could say the same of some of the other alcoholics we knew.

The early days of the Pembina oil field are hard to forget, with over twelve-hundred active rigs in the area—the "largest oil field (in area) in the world." Our clinic saw countless accidents. I think the record was fourteen Workers' Compensation Board accidents in one day, and I'm sure the other clinic in town was equally busy. I got to know many of the specialists in Edmonton, including the famous Dr. Harry Weinlos. In fact, I stayed with him once for a sleepless forty-eight hours as I followed him on his rounds. He drove a beat-up old car, to the utter shame of his more conventional relatives, and I spent some time push-starting it in the arctic cold, freezing my ears in the process. For the next few years, Harry Weinlos' first words to me, whenever we met, were "How are your ears?"

Dr. Weinlos was not the only specialist who helped me make the transition from jack-of-all-trades in Africa to general practitioner in rural Canada—a very different proposition from a G.P. in England. In fact, I started practice in Drayton Valley with considerable fear and trembling, since I had been without any colleague to critique my skills for a dozen years or more. As it turned out, doctoring in an isolated African setting was in many ways perfect training for Canadian practice ninety miles from the nearest specialist help.

Dr. Hugh Maclure

Those were the days of mud and gravel roads, when we all wore "Drayton Valley Oxfords" summer and winter. The main street was lined with mud-caked trucks and nineteen-foot-long cars with homicidal hood ornaments and cracked windshields. In due course we acquired a Mini-Morris for short trips and house-calls, and quickly learned why such tiny cars are not fashionable in Western Canada. In thirty-below weather, the rear wheels would not have time to thaw out during the short trip from house to clinic on the ice-covered road. This gave many opportunities for nearby smart alecks to practice their wit by asking why my rear wheels were not revolving, as well, of course, as such questions as "Where's the one for the other foot?"

Before a vet came to stay, most of the doctors in town treated animals as well as people. One morning, a colleague sadly told me he had lost his first maternity case in the night. Before I could express my sympathy, he added, "But the calf is doing fine." In Africa, Sunday was emergency Caesarian section day, but in the oil field, it seemed to be the time for anesthetizing dogs of all shapes and sizes in order to extract porcupine quills from their muzzles. I learned that a seventy-pound German Shepherd takes three times the human dose of Pentothal to put him out. Many other headlines come to mind. Apart from "The Cat's Birthday" (more about which later), there was "The Beaver with Chronic Fatigue Syndrome," "The Trumpeter Swan with Rheumatoid Arthritis(?)" and so on.

We had a small skid-shack in the trees by Wabamun Lake and used to go out there on days off. This taught us something of the mysteries of Alberta summer weather. If I had the after-noon off, Sunny Alberta would live up to its name until noon, and then the clouds would move in as we drove the thirty miles to the lake. In spite of this, our memories of our lakeshore retreat are very happy ones. We made a pre-fab "Enterprise"-class sailing dinghy, a project that took about six times as long as the instructions proclaimed! To this day, the smell of swamp poplars and pine needles evoke some wonderful memories.

In due course our three boys went to the University of Alberta, where they divided their time between study, swimming and gymnastics. One year, I, David, Paul and Andrew all took our bronze medallion tests together. It was a great relief to have the test over and not find myself humiliated by comparison with my sons!

Two of our sons got involved in canoeing, and our eldest, along with two others from Drayton Valley, was in the Alberta team that took part in the centennial race from Rocky Mountain House to Montreal in 1967, traversing in reverse the route of the original *voyageurs* along the waterways of Canada. They paddled over three thousand miles that summer, with only eighteen miles of portages. Our son wore out six pairs of jeans sliding from one side of the big Chestnut canoe to the other, and earned enough from provincial and federal grants to put himself through University for the next year doing so. Alberta came in third behind B.C. and Manitoba.

Many Canadian doctors will tell you that the years in the '50s, '60s and '70s were heyday years in general practice. In addition, for us, they came in between years in Africa, in conditions as far removed from the rough-and-ready affluence of oil patch Alberta as one could possibly imagine. For myself, perhaps more than for the other members of my family, the "best of times" far outweighed "the worst of times." Particularly was this true in three areas.

Firstly, as I have said, those were the golden years of rural practice in Alberta. When I see the obstacles—political, economic and professional—with which young doctors have to put up today, I thank God for allowing me to practice in the Dinosaur era, when physicians with experience had great freedom to take responsibility for cases which today would have to be referred. I realize that there are good reasons, with the increase in hi-tech procedures, for many of the restrictions put on family doctors in the new century. I'm just glad I got to practice when I did.

During much of our time in Drayton Valley, the average age of the town was ten years. I delivered over 1300 babies there, and for several years, the hospital had the lowest perinatal mortality of any facility of comparable size in the province. I still frequently meet some of my "babies," or *their* children, in The Bay or Sears in Edmonton.

One could go on and on with medical anecdotes, but I do not have the advantage of a vet, such as James Herriot, who can write about his patients without fear of revealing confidential medical information. Of course, fitting medical practice into a life with many other interests was a problem, too. We used to go to Jasper for the day to ski, leaving at five a.m. and returning after the ski-lift shut down, getting home about nine in the evening. This made a long day, and on one occasion, it was longer still.

It was four a.m., and the phone rang calling me to the hospital to help a colleague with a case of ruptured spleen in a pregnant woman. I had planned that day to go skiing at Jasper with my next-door neighbour, a genial oil man with O-negative blood. We got him up, took off two pints of his unique blood, and got the spleen removed after a touchy hour in the OR. We skied vigorously for six hours and my friend suffered no ill effects, judging by my efforts to keep up with him. The patient made a good recovery minus her spleen, going on to give birth to a healthy baby four months later.

To return to the subject. Secondly, we found Drayton Valley to be a very warm and friendly place, though at first we had to overcome the assumption that "Limeys" were likely to be snobs with an incomprehensible sense of humour. We made a host of new friends, and many of them were promptly transferred to Calgary or Texas or some other area of the oil industry. My wife became active in the Toast-Mistress organization and hospital auxiliary, as well as coping with the demands of three active boys and a husband whose mealtimes were unpredictable. We started a community choir and sang "pop" cantatas at Christmas and Easter, even tackling bits of *Messiah*, though accompanying George Frederick Handel on the spinet organ is not to be recommended. This choir was one of the highlights of our years in the oil patch.

Two of our sons took part in various canoe races in the N. Saskatchewan river, apart from the Centennial race, and in those years we drove many miles along the back roads around Drayton Valley, the long-suffering car loaded with canoes. We put the paddlers into the water and picked them up later downstream. Before the centennial race, I sometimes jogged in the evenings with two of the team members. They would burden themselves with twelve pounds of nails apiece, and wear rig boots. I panted to keep up with them, stripped to the bare essentials. Later, two of our sons and another paddler from Drayton Valley took part in the Quebec ice carnival, crossing the half-frozen St. Lawrence River more or less in the boat or on the ice-floes. Our eldest son went on to take part in this crazy race ten times.

Thirdly, we were active in the evangelical community. We started a regular weekly home Bible-study group, and when we left in 1969, there were ten at least going on in the town.

When we left Drayton Valley, all three boys were nearing the end of their courses in dentistry, medicine and teacher training. I did two short residences at the City Hospital. The next year, we went to Uganda, and were there when Sergeant Idi Amin made his overnight leap up the promotion ladder to Field-Marshal.

Since that time, we have done several short spells back there in practice, and our teacher son has worked in one of the schools there for twenty-five years or so. Our time in the oil-patch was an immensely satisfying and significant part of our Canadian experience.

The Addictive List-Making Syndrome

ONE night recently, unable to sleep, I got up and fumbled my way to my desk. Bleary-eyed, I began to make a list of all the things which had been chasing themselves round and round in my head like mice on a treadmill. Having unloaded the chaotic thoughts on to paper, I returned to bed and sleep came quickly.

Here was a classical example of the Addictive List-Making Syndrome, or ALMS, and anyone coming to my desk and surfing through the smorgasbord of papers, bills, statements, advertisements appeals and coffee-cup stained envelopes and photos of my great-grandchildren would soon find other evidence of the condition. Many lists would come to light, scribbled on "Post-It slips," prescription forms and the backs of bank-statements. Illegible and/or incomprehensible messages such as "lettuce," "pay Albert," "Gaviscon on sale," "SS notes for the 24th," "new chain and valve caps," etc., would remind you that a patient with ALMS lived here.

The above sentence, containing as it does three lists, partially explains the relevance of ALMS to the subject of writing; but before developing this theme, the various manifestations of the condition should be mentioned. All can be present in one individual at the same time.

The earliest evidence of ALMS in my own life is lost in obscurity, because for the first few years of my life I was illiterate. However, by the time I was in school, the most benign of the three strains was already well developed. This was ALMS(M), the *M*-strain being list-making as an aid to memory. On my note-books, scraps of paper or even the back of my hand could be found such jottings as "check on axolotl," "revise *ranunculus repens*," "new puncture kit," "Barbadoes stamps," and always among the notes and sometimes obscuring them were caricatures of my friends or of the French or chemistry teachers.

ALMS(M) was also evident in our days in West Africa. I remember a trek on foot in a heavy tropical rainstorm. On changing, I came across a sodden notebook in a pocket and quickly copied the list it contained while it was still legible. It consisted of language notes in three dialects—"mouse-trap" (Temne), "eclipse of the moon" (Koranko), "turn a somersault" (Limba) and others. Soon afterwards, I wrote—with apologies to G.K. Chesterton—an article entitled "Pages from a Wet Note-book," which was later published.

The second and most malignant strain of the list-making syndrome is ALMS(S); i.e., list-making as a substitute for action. In the tropics, this dread strain flourishes like dandelions in summer, encouraged by the heat and humidity. It flourished on mission deputation tours as well, as we did little but talk about our future plans for several months without actually putting them into practice.

In Africa, the evidence for the existence of the *S*-strain was found in the countless lists I (and others) made: "learn Arabic," "fence in the banana patch," "learn more Limba proverbs," etc., none of which I actually got around to doing. In fact, the absence of "a round tuit" was felt to some extent throughout our twenty years overseas. In the end, I postponed list-making until the evenings when laziness was at its maximum. This way, I would wake in the cooler hours of the morning with the duties of the day already listed. Without such a list, we would never have been able to translate the New Testament in the time allotted.

The third strain of ALMS is the "W" strain, list-making as an incentive to writing. Many articles published recently started as ideas scribbled semi-legibly on whatever was handy—for instance, "A Prolonged Grief," "The Missionary Kid Minefield," "Clinical Study: a Case of Chronically Happy Marriage" and "The Addictive List-making Syndrome."

ALMS(W) continues its influence after the subject has been chosen. Lists are made of alternative opening sentences, illustrations to use, how to treat the subject (as an infection? A psychological curiosity? A congenital defect?), things to emphasize, alternative endings, and as the advertisements say, much much more.

I have started a new ALMS(W) list. On it is a reminder to try to find the list I made of subjects for future articles. I want to cross off the last item.

ive Me That Old Time Religion, Occasionally

Reprinted from Christian Week, *Nov. 2000*

"WE are seriously thinking of leaving this church and going somewhere with reverent worship. All this clapping and drumming and noisy banal choruses... it's absolutely awful!" My Scottish friend, usually a man of few words, was beginning to simmer like a 747 after a transatlantic flight.

I could sympathize with his frustration. For me, clapping is for Pavarotti, Gretzky and other performers, not for the player of an offertory. Applause after I have played one myself makes me cringe, lest God do to me what He did to Herod Agrippa. Cheering is for the Edmonton Oilers, not for Christians emerging from the baptismal tank. Eighty years of conditioning make it hard for me to believe that clapping today means exactly what saying "Amen" meant to previous generations. Glorifying a performer is surely not the same as affirming God's truth.

In the meantime, Angus, my friend, becomes more and more convinced that noise, saxophones and choruses are sure evidence that the last of the last days are upon us. He links to the change in worship format the undoubted slide in numbers at the mid-week prayer meeting, and the diminishing (he thinks) Bible knowledge of church members. *"When the Son of Man comes, will He find faith on the earth?"* (Luke 18:8 NIV).

Part of me agrees, yet I am not entirely certain my instinctive dislike of what is happening on Sunday mornings stems from my superior Christian discernment. Perhaps—hideous thought!—it's largely because of my unwillingness to pay the price of worshipping with people of other ages and other cultures. My age, race and upbringing encourage me to concentrate on the negative aspects of the new worship service; a knee-jerk reaction, in fact. But is not the Holy Spirit Lord also of my reflexes? Perhaps I should suspend judgement and spend some time looking at both sides of the question.

The negatives hit me immediately in the eye (and ear). So little silence! *"Let all the earth be silent before Him"* (Habakkuk 2:20 NIV), *"In quietness and confidence shall be your strength* (Isaiah 30:15 KJV)," *"Be still and know that I am God* (Psalm 46:10 NIV)"—such verses imply a worship atmosphere which is immediately destroyed by a young man in a T-shirt pounding a drum or swallowing a microphone. As for a piano tinkling while the pastor prays! Surely I am not the only one who, while struggling to identify with what is being said, fights an overwhelming urge to tiptoe down the aisle and strangle the pianist?

And then there are the choruses! I love choruses around a campfire, where they seem to be entirely appropriate. It's the almost complete exclusion of hymns that is the problem. Nor do I appreciate standing to sing the same verse of a chorus five times while my elderly inter-vertebral discs grind painfully, and one suspects, audibly. Again, having all the words of song and Scripture up on an overhead may be great for teaching a new chorus, but it hardly encourages one to bring or use a Bible. Besides, what about the $10,000 the church spent on hymn books?

Recently we attended an old-fashioned hymn singalong with 1500 others in a large evangelical church. When choices were asked for, a voice requested "A Mighty Fortress Is Our God." Hardly anyone knew it. Surely the Rapture and Great Tribulation must be just around the corner!

I could go on, but after a cup of tea and advice from my wife to cool down, I will turn to the positive side of the new worship style.

First, new format churches are awash with youth. We asked a friend about the service in her church and she proudly claimed that they still used the piano and organ, and sang from a hymn book, using very few choruses. "How big is your youth group?" we tactlessly asked. "Well, we are mostly older people, but we have a few kids who come with their parents," was the reply. Exactly.

As for repetition, I was discussing this with a grandson the other day. "Your songs have repetition, too" he said. I argued this unsuccessfully for a bit and then got to thinking. In Handel's *Messiah*, there is more repetition than one would ever hear in a youth meeting—for instance, the words "all we like sheep" are repeated eight times, and "we have turned" thirty-four times, at last count. And the same could be said for most of the other arias and choruses in it, and what's more, we enjoy it!

Having recently spent a month in a B.C. city with many large evangelical churches, I realize the dinosaurs have nothing much to complain about in our church in Edmonton. One of the morning services expressly caters for those who, like me, hate progress. We have a large youth group of all ages, hundreds being touched through outreach endeavours, a program in the local schools, summer camp programs involving both church and 'outside' kids. When our seniors had a few days at camp last year, the youth group gave up time to lead our singing. Not exactly the songs we had had in mind, but their enthusiasm and willingness to serve were unquestioned.

Secondly, when Paul wrote of Christ abolishing the barriers between various classes of people, he could truthfully have added "young or old" to the list. Why did I find this harder to accept in West Canada than West Africa? In village churches overseas, we often met in a shelter, sitting on boards six inches off the ground, with dogs and chickens as part of the congregation. We sang songs using a five-tone scale in one of three languages to the accompaniment of teenaged boys beating kerosene tins to death. None of the distracting and critical thoughts which run through my head in Canada ever disturbed my worship there on Sundays. It all seemed appropriate and entirely compatible with our aim to encourage an indigenous African form of worship.

At first in Africa I had used an accordion, which certainly drew crowds to village services. As the church gradually developed, they discarded most of the clumsy translations of "good old" hymns made by earlier missionaries and began to make up their own Christian songs, with their own tone scale, rhythms and words—a move resisted by some of the older missionaries! I soon discarded my instrument as being too foreign and incapable of accompanying the West African antiphonal singing.

Another awful thought has struck me. While priding myself on not being racist in Africa, have I become a Christian snob in Canada unawares?

There are many other sides to what is happening in our Sunday services, all of them tending to rattle my comfort-zone cage. I am beginning to understand why C.S. Lewis liked "boredom" in worship. His criticism of extemporary prayer applies to the new worship form. It calls upon you "to carry on a critical and devotional activity at the same moment—two things hardly possible" (*Letters of C.S. Lewis,* edited by W.H. Lewis, Geoffrey Bles Ltd, 1966).

Traditional church services I remember from my youth had two priceless benefits. The Bible, both Old and New Testaments, was read every Sunday, and prayers, however formal, were made for three subjects overlooked very frequently in our worship today—namely the government, the worldwide church and the unevangelised world with its needs, both spiritual and physical. These do not appear to be high-priority issues for intercession today. We mostly pray for ourselves.

So, some of the regular elements in our Sunday morning services are disappearing like the black-footed ferret. The sanctuary choir is struggling for survival, being choked out of existence by multiplying weeknight meetings that leave no time for the regular weekly practices on which it depends. Yet, the evening meetings themselves are often signs of new life and outreach in the church. Home Bible studies flourish and at each there is a time when people pray together, so I do not regard the extinction of the mid-week prayer meeting necessarily as a disaster.

Of course, I also miss the deeply spiritual words and rich harmonies of some (not all) of our traditional hymns, but culture and education are dangerous guides when seeking a Christian attitude, providing as they do a perfect medium for growing the virulent virus of Christian snobbery

Sometimes sanctuary choirs rise from the dead in December and go into a convulsion of effort, which I suspect may occasionally be prompted by a desire to keep up with the Joneses' church. The congregation with the most live donkeys in its Christmas program wins.

Having separate services for older and younger worshippers pleases many, but tends to break up families on Sunday mornings and perhaps harden concrete attitudes (and burn out pastors).

Is the modern free-and-easy service going to do what its opposite, cold formalism, did to the church in Europe since the Reformation? Probably not. Drums and guitars are being used to bring young people to Christ, and the church in Europe was killed by secular humanism in its own ranks, not by formalism alone.

My generation tends to face youth with fear and incomprehension, not understanding the impact the multiple choices, information overload and agnostic teachers are having on them. I try to see what is under their reversed baseball caps, with a big assist from my grandchildren. Meanwhile, we hang in there, worship as best we can and make a joyful noise when humanly possible.

Beware the Word Hijackers

From "Physician" *Magazine, July-August 2001.*

MY favourite Flanders and Swann song tells of the British Bedstead Men who, working at dead of night, keep England's lily ponds, streams and little lakes well stocked with a supply of oil-drums, truck tires, old boots and broken brass bedsteads.

Taking my cue from these two marvellous entertainers, I'm writing my own song about another secret society, the Word Hijackers. These furtive creatures kidnap well-defined, even honourable words, descending on them like wasps at a picnic (to change the metaphor), and with an assist from the news media, corrupt the original meaning—all unsuspected by the public. Once altered, the words become meaningless without extensive footnotes.

I have come to avoid the hijackers' targets altogether. *Gay, fundamentalist, and homophobic* are already on my list of words thus rendered useless, and *tolerance* is on the way out. Today I am adding another, *holism.* Sometime after the 1952 edition of the Shorter Oxford Dictionary was printed, this word and its adjectival form, *holistic*, appeared. According to Webster, it's been part of the English vernacular since 1926, and it is defined by a meaning identical to that of the good old word, *whole*.

Suzan Walter, president of the American Holistic Health Association describes *holism* thus—"It starts with the (whole person) philosophy that recognizes the interrelationship between all aspects of who we are and the world we live in…. Achieving health is an ongoing personal journey toward a goal of functioning at our very best level possible" (*Resource Guide to Alternative Health*, HealthInform, New York).

Sentiments as old as the hills. Who could take exception to them?

Several universities now have established graduate programs in holistic health care, presumably as a reaction against the cold, scientific and impersonal approach to the patient more and more taught in medical schools.

But beware! The hijackers have taken *holism* captive.

Take, for instance, Gerda Boyesen—a biodynamic psychotherapist who, employing a flood of postmodern and undefined (and undefinable) New Age psychobabble, carries the meaning of *holism* into that Wonderland where postmoderns manufacture their own truth. With a smattering of ideas from Freud, Jung and William Reich, to name a few, Boyesen scatters like confetti such phrases as "primary personality," "cosmic energy," "self-regulation," "balancing earth and spiritual energies," and others, until the mind boggles.

Working closely with the Eastern concept of life-energy, she is into meridians, chakras and auras. She claims that the gut is a Freudian "id" canal, processing not only material food, but also going to work on spiritual and emotional nourishment, helping us to deal with the serving of circumstances that come our way and eliminating what is not best for us—all of which can be detected and controlled by listening to the abdomen with a stethoscope. (Personally I've always suspected that a good portion of baked beans causes one's bowels to vibrate in sync with the vibes of the universe.)

Boyesen also refers to ancient Greek connotations of the caduceus, the snake-on-a-stick emblem on your Med-Alert card. To her, it represents the twin influences of the cerebrospinal fluid and the alimentary canal entwined about the median lines of our bodies (*Training Prospectus—2000*, Institute of Biodynamic Psychology and Psychotherapy, London). Nothing could more clearly show the gulf between the postmodern ideas of holism and the Christian concept of *wholeness*, which relates the caduceus to Moses' life-saving serpent in the wilderness.

In Canada, the caduceus is worn as a badge by physicians who belong to the "Hippocratic Register"—a fellowship of health workers who are committed to the modern interpretation of the Hippocratic Oath rather than to the Canadian Medical Association's filleted version, which has taken most of the ethical content out of the oath, including the promise not to perform abortions.

Speaking of wholeness, the Old Testament sums it up in Proverbs 3:7,8—

> *Do not be wise in your own eyes; fear the Lord and shun evil. This will bring health to your body and nourishment to your bones* (NIV).

Similarly, the apostle Paul left little room for debate when he wrote,

> *May God Himself, the God of peace, sanctify you through and through. May your whole spirit, soul and body be kept blameless at the coming of our Lord Jesus Christ*" (1 Thessalonians 5:23, NIV).

In both Old and New Testament teaching, the emphasis is on being right with God first. Wholeness, self-esteem, fulfillment and a sense of identity all come as *fringe benefits*.

The word-hijackers are doing us one good turn, however. They are restoring to the word *Christian* some of the original contempt and hatred that prompted the coining of the word in first-century Antioch. That in itself should stiffen our spines and cause us to hold our heads high. After all, to be called to share some of the trials of the early church is no mean honour.

Ten Years of Bike for Bibles

IN 1992, about a dozen cyclists rode for a week through the mountains in that part of Alberta bordering on British Columbia. Among their number were two or three Australians. Each rider had sponsors supporting the work of the Canadian Bible Society. The Aussie riders had come to Canada to show the Canadians the ropes, as they had developed "Bike for Bibles" rides down under and were anxious to spread this fundraising event to other countries.

This was the beginning of an annual cycle ride of about 800 kilometres by a Canadian team and it has now raised over $300,000 for the spread of the written Word of God throughout the world. In its tenth year (2002), it is appropriate to look back on these glorious weeks in the mountains. I had the privilege of riding in every one of them, providing Scriptures and other materials for Russia, Colombia, Brazil, Africa, Madagascar, India, Egypt, and other places.

My own involvement in Bike for Bibles was by accident (sort of). A sixteen-year-old grandson with an innocent expression on his face asked me one day, in April 1993, if I'd like to go for a little ride with the church youth group later in the year. I said, "Yes, of course," picturing a day trip of perhaps 25 km in which I would be able to show these whipper-snappers there was life in the old carcass yet.

Two days later, I found I had committed myself to 800 km in a week. A battle between my pride and my discretion ensued, with discretion winning by a short head. However, I next heard that the whole caper was to be a sponsored ride for the Canadian Bible Society, an organization I had long supported. In fact, I had done Scripture translation for the British branch of the same society before we came to Canada in 1956. This turned the scales and I proceeded, in fear and trembling, to train.

At the beginning of the last week in July, we gathered in Calgary and eyed each other nervously. I noted the young muscles and hi-tech bikes of my comrades, and felt that sinking feeling familiar to all those who have sat for final medical and other exams. I hung on to Psalm 121, which assured me the Lord would take care of my coming in as well as my going out, and Psalm 139, which promised He would also take care of my probably painful down-sitting and uprising.

We traveled to Revelstoke in a school bus which accompanied us all the way on our journey, carrying our bed-rolls, etc., while a big trailer took our bikes to our starting point. We had fish and chips at Canmore on the way, and this became a ritual we repeated every year we traveled this particular route. (Some years we started in Calgary and went south.)

At Revelstoke, we stayed overnight in the basement of the Alliance church, and very quickly noticed there was only one bathroom for each sex. After a fairly good night when we were able to identify, but not isolate, the snorers, we assembled, had a short devotional, gave our war-cry of "By our spokes God speaks!" and set off. I soon realized that I was not going to be the one who delayed the whole team and promptly lost my fears.

Each day was divided into four sections of 25-30 km each, with refreshments or lunch in between. A team of five or six "roadies" kept us well hydrated and nourished, drove accompanying vehicles and cooked when necessary. After a few years, the fame of our cook had spread and it was generally acknowledged that the "Rocky Mountain Ride" team was the best-fed group doing Bike for Bibles in Canada. (By the year 2000, there were several other teams in other parts of Canada.) I have never lost weight doing Bike for Bibles, but have happily had it redistributed a bit. Also, I come home every year with an appetite like a bear after hibernation.

By now, the individual rides of the last ten years tend to merge together in my memory. Twice I have had a grandchild on the trip with me, and my wife has been a roadie three times. Once my older brother, visiting us from England after spending forty-four years in Uganda with AIM, came as an observer. He had done translations for the Bible society in the Lugbara, Acholi, Kakwa and Alur languages of central Africa. He thoroughly enjoyed the journey, though we had not realized his poor state of health. I remember one awful moment in the basement of a church in Banff when he went black in the face and collapsed while trying to blow up his sleeping bag. He recovered soon and continued the journey next day to Calgary, and claimed he had had one of the best weeks of his life.

In 1994, our fifteen-year-old granddaughter came with a friend. After the first day, from Golden to Invermere, about 115 km, both of them individually wanted to quit and go home, but neither would be the first to give in. By the third day they were doing well, and at the end I was hard-put to keep up with them. At Creston, our granddaughter caught the wheel of the bike in front and crashed at slow speed. She was unhurt, but her water-bottle spilled, splashing blood-red Kool-Aid over herself and the roadside. This caused quite a stir until a proper diagnosis was made.

Medical assistance was not required on that occasion, but I have given out scores of Advil pills, eye drops, bandages and Gaviscon tablets, and taken a biker to a local hospital a time or two for possible appendicitis or fractured collarbones. I've sewed up lacerations by the roadside a couple of times, and my own blood has stained the Trans-Canada Highway, though in small quantities only. Altogether, in about 1,800 man (and woman) hours of cycling, we've had no serious accidents and very few minor ones, praise the Lord!

As the years went by, we learned to form small "peletons," *a la* Tour de France, in which a group of riders of similar ability get into line, each about two feet (in the Tour, it's more like six inches!) behind the biker in front. Every quarter of a mile or so, there is a shout of "Rotate!," and the back rider comes to the front, rotating clockwise under the instructions of an Australian expert. Actually, we should have gone anti-clockwise, rotating *away* from the verge of the road. The Aussie had forgotten he was not in his home country where they bike on the left as well as upside down.

Drafting helps tremendously, especially on the flat stretches. Some of us found it hard to stay with the peleton up the hills and we dropped behind, catching up again on the downhill or level. The spirit of fellowship and mutual support was beautifully in evidence on these occasions. I was helped along for many miles by considerate stronger bikers who drafted me in a two-rider peleton. How beautiful upon the mountains are the feet (and backside) of the rider just ahead of one's front wheel!

At night we stayed in churches and soon learned to memorize the route to the bathroom before the lights went out. It often involved a flight of stairs and a trek through a passage or two choked with bikes with shin-destroying pedals! About half the time, though, my gray hairs earned me a billet with some hospitable church member. There I could wallow in a hot bath and sleep on a featherbed, while my comrades ate their hearts out on a church basement floor. It was a chance to get some laundry done, too.

Our evenings were highlights as we met in the host church for singing, sharing, worshipping the Lord of the Bible and cementing friendships. Sometimes, too, there was a chance to visit a hot pool.

As the years went by, I upgraded the bike in small increments to compensate for my aging powers and the fact that the movement of the earth's tectonic plates was making the long hills longer and higher. My twenty-five-year-old Apollo had twelve gears and I soon altered that to eighteen, which helped, particularly on the twelve-km hill out of Radium through Yoho parkway. I had already put speedbars on to give my arthritic back a change of position occasionally. Next year, I found with delight I had a genuine excuse for the extravagance of a new bike—the Apollo had a crack in its frame! So, goodbye, Kawasaki, welcome Marinoni—a medium-priced (i.e., under $2,000!) but personally measured bike with twenty-four gears and wheels and cranks which I could not hear complaining when I freewheeled. Two years later, I changed to "spuds" (against advice), i.e., special boots which clipped on to the pedals. They have made a great difference once I was used to them, and in spite of dire predictions, I've only had a few minor crashes at slow speed.

Finally, two years ago I discarded my old saddle, which was entirely held together with duct tape, and came up with a much lighter and more modern one with a split in the middle which has made the last day or two of each trip a lot more comfortable.

Now I've reached the limits of affordable upgrading and I'm on my own!

Five times now, our last day has consisted of a fast run in from Banff with a strong tail wind, which enables even the slowest of us to keep up a 30- to 35-kilometre per hour clip. It is a situation where fatigue, the knowledge of once more having "made" it and the wind-assisted euphoria of speed causes me to praise the Lord for His blessings to me, remembering that my bike alone cost more than the annual income of most of the people who will be getting the Scriptures we are providing. In fact, as I fly along, I find this last day a psalm-making experience—

> *O give thanks unto the LORD for He is good,*
> *For His mercy endures for ever.*
> *To Him that alone made the Rocky Mountains,*
> *For His mercy endures for ever.*
> *To Him that made titanium and carbon fiber for the wealthy,*
> *For His mercy endures for ever.*
> *And chrome-molybdenum for the humble and poor,*
> *For His mercy endures for ever.*
> *To Him that provided kevlar for the tires,*
> *For His mercy endures for ever.*
> *And twelve to thirty two-cassettes for the endless hills;*
> *For His mercy endures for ever… and so on…*

At Calgary, a great welcome and meal awaits us, then the final ceremony and fond farewells until next time. The team—without age barriers or denominational jealousies—scatters, and the committee begins to plan next year's ride. What wonderful friendships (and one marriage at least) have been made during these ten exciting weeks. Thank You, LORD!

Our trip in 2002 marked the tenth year of exclusively Canadian Bike for Bibles rides. To wind things up, there was a barbecue in one of the parks in Calgary, followed by a program. A song was sung to the tune of "Home on the Range":

Oh give me a road with a strict highway code,
Where the Raleighs and Canondales play.
Where never is heard a discouraging word,
And the trucks do not roar past each day.

> *"Bike for Bibles" we state.*
> *"By our spokes God speaks" is our cry.*
> *We all will rotate and we won't dehydrate,*
> *And our tires will not let the air out!*

Oh give me a space for my bed-roll to place,
Not too far from the washroom is right.
Where I can repose with no feet on my nose,
And my friends are not snoring all night.

> *"Bike for Bibles" we cry,*
> *"By our spokes God speaks" every day.*
> *To keep up we try as the mountains fly by,*
> *And the traffic makes all watch and pray.*

Oh give me an hour to relax in the shower
With my soap and shampoo close at hand.
Then restoring my power with our host's sweet and sour

Dr. Hugh Maclure

I apply the sun-screen where I'm tanned.

> *"Bike for Bibles" again,*
> *"By our spokes God speaks" every year.*
> *Next summer I'll train till my legs feel the pain,*
> *And if God allows I'll be there.*

Oh give me a heart that is glad to take part
In the spread of the Word of the Lord.
Where we joyfully share the Good News everywhere
Until all lands and nations have heard.

> *"Bike for Bibles" we sing,*
> *"By our spokes God speaks" we declare.*
> *With our "roadies" as one 'til the journey is done,*
> *We will help sow the Seed everywhere.*

In Sierra Leone Before the Civil War

Adapted from Letters From the White Man's Grave *by Dr H.L. Maclure, Credo Publishing Corp. 1994, reprinted 1996.*

I am at present on trek, sitting in the traditional missionary manner under a mango tree, with my camping gear on the veranda of a thatched-roof house nearby. The beautiful mile-high Yara Mountains rise in front of me as the flies and other assorted insects buzz excitedly around, planning their next meal. The scene only lacks, hopefully, the missionary-eating lion crouching in the elephant grass and the green mamba, in the tree above, waiting to strike.

Several things stand out on this journey. Preaching the gospel where it has rarely, if ever, been heard before; actually feeling cold in the mornings in these mountain foothills, the blind man's face lighting up as he was told that, God willing, he would see again; the circle of Koranko people listening every night to the story of redemption; the six-hour daily walk through the farms and forest; and, of course, the crowded clinics which often last all day.

This wild northeastern Sierra Leone country, of elephants and the rare pygmy hippo, abounds with the sounds, sights and smells of West Africa, which eventually seem to become absorbed into one's very bones. Particularly it is the smells which will never be forgotten—the bad ones more than compensated for by the odour of dried fish and palm-oil, rancid butter in the hair of the Fula women and the sickly sweet smell from an unidentified blossom at the edge of the forest.

Then there are the sounds! Doves of various kinds call in many rhythms and keys. We walk to the cadence of the opening bars of Beethoven's fifth symphony, *ku-ku-ku-kuuu, ku-ku-ku-kuuu*, only to have it replaced by a dove which starts slowly and then accelerates to a frantic finish—*kuuu-kuuu-kuu-ku-kukukuku*! Nothing evokes homesickness more in the heart of an old "west-coaster" than the sound of doves in the background of a nature film about Africa on TV.

Another bird emits a sharp screech, repeated ten or eleven times. They say if she cries an even number of times, a man will be the next to die in the close-by village; if an uneven number, then it will be a woman.

The "nearly-dead" bird, with her tail so long and heavy she can barely make it to the next tree, thrashes wildly through the tops of the elephant grass before resting exhausted. (Those who believe she arrived by a process of unplanned naturalistic evolution have trouble with this bird!) The bush-fowl stands on his stump in the farm, calling despairingly for his stumpy little tail to be restored; and in the high forest, the red colobus monkeys howl and the black colobus' swing their long white tails and peer down through their beards at the intruders 200 feet below.

High up in the cottonwood trees, a great gray hornbill arrives with a noisy wingbeat like an asthmatic helicopter. She lands clumsily on a limb and begins to wail in grief for her grand-mother, whose corpse she carries in the coffin on top of her beak. Crouched in the grass at the forest edge, the west African hare (Brer Rabbit of legendary fame) dreams of ways to outwit the hippopotamus and escape from the hyena (Brer Wolf).

Amid this medley of noise, myth and natural history, the disturbing hullabaloo emitted by the gray plantain eater—a species of mountain turacao—most represents to me the hilly jungles where the Koranko people live. One of their proverbs says, "If you don't like the call of the plantain eater (*kerengbongbon*), don't make your farm near the high forest"—the African equivalent of "If you can't stand the heat, stay out of the kitchen." The description of this bird, with minor adjustments, fits the Koranko people themselves: "Medium large, with crest on the back of the head, usually seen in pairs or small parties keeping mainly near the trees. They fly in single file and eat a variety of vegetable foods. A noisy species with a wide range of calls" (from *Birds of the West African Town and Garden*, by Elgood, Longmans and Green, 1960). Young Koranko boys even cut their hair with a crest on the back of the head. It was because we loved the Koranko people that we "made our farm" where they lived.

Dr. Hugh Maclure

At night we hear the bush-baby, the long-tailed big-eyed gulago, with his soulful baby face and human expression. He laments mournfully to himself in the darkness because, though his hands, feet and face are human, he has been cursed with a tail like a mere monkey. At daybreak, as the white egrets float through the mist over the rice farms, that bright little finch, the bulbul, wakes us with repeated cries of "Quick doctor, quick!" And when that fails to produce action, an exasperated "Fetch the ambulance" follows. Later he attempts to calm himself down by whistling a theme from Beethoven's Piano Sonata Opus 52 in F minor (the "Apassionata").

Treks such as this bring a welcome change from the hassle of doctoring and building simultaneously. A nurse is carrying on in my absence with my wife's help. The nurse's training as a dental technician relieves me of much of the work in the one area of medicine that I detest! She also does a lot of the triage work at the clinic, leaving me to deal with her referrals and round up sand, gravel and lumber for the new hospital we are building.

We get boards from a saw-pit west of the town where two men have been ripping up a mahogany log with a double-ended saw, the boss standing on top and sawing down, with much shouting and yelling of instructions, while his unfortunate assistant saws upwards from below, his mouth, eyes and ears full of sawdust.

Before I came on this trip, I left a stout Koranko (rather a rarity in this lanky tribe) digging a stout well; so stout, in fact, that it will probably have to be cemented when I get back, to prevent a cave-in. Getting a bag of cement into the town involves two carriers walking thirty miles, and catching a truck for another thirty miles, to reach our mission headquarters. The bag of cement then has to be divided into two. They pick up the mail and bring the cement back, carrying it on their heads. The complete operation takes the best part of a week.

A party of patients is approaching, walking single file and keeping near the trees. I can hear them at a distance, because they are a noisy tribe with a variety of calls. I doubt whether they've ever had a doctor in their village before.

S*hadowlands*—A Review of the Film

SOME people arouse such conflicting partisan opinion that no film on their lives can ever please everybody. Two such men died recently. One was John F. Kennedy. The other was C.S. Lewis, the "apostle to the agnostics." He called himself a "lapsed atheist," and warned the young materialist to be very careful what he read if he wished to maintain his or her faith. *Shadowlands* is a beautifully made film about the circumstances of his marriage to Joy Davidman, an American divorcee, and their brief life together before she died of cancer. Romance and drama of a high order is sensitively acted by Anthony Hopkins and Debra Winger.

In this film, Lewis's early years, his brilliant career as scholar and teacher, his conversion to basic Christianity and his emergence as one of the world's most powerful, learned and lucid writers witnessing to the intellectual post-Christian world—all these essentials in the make up of the C.S. Lewis story are omitted or barely touched upon.

It is perhaps unreasonable to complain that a film about the latter years of a man's life is not about the earlier years of that life, but admirers of C.S. Lewis's writing may well feel that the real man is missing in *Shadowlands*. The actual Dr. Lewis was the most sought-after lecturer at Oxford (and later, Cambridge) University, the brilliant scholar, the writer of inspiring and lucid English, the most formidable advocate of politically-incorrect Christianity in the ongoing intellectual debate that is part and parcel of English university life. However, in this film, instead of this terse, remorselessly logical and clear-thinking author and teacher, we are left with a rather pathetic and impractical university professor, living in a "shadowland" of his own making to protect himself from cruel reality.

C.S. Lewis had a "shadowland," alright, but it was very different. It was the shadowland of the Romantic Idealist—more, not less, real than reality—the realm of the elusive Divine Vision, the glimpse of the ideal and heavenly country, the memory of Eden. In fact, it was the lingering hint of Paradise Lost, which Christians are beginning to regain through faith in Christ Himself, the Ultimate Reality. The feeling of pressure under this "weight of glory" ran like a thread through all the writings of C.S. Lewis after his conversion, and indeed there was a foretaste of it even when he was still an agnostic. (*"Surprised By Joy,"* a personal account of his very reluctant conversion, is full of hints concerning this "vision.")

This is the shadowy and fleeting glimpse of a world more real than the one in which we live that Lewis has been able to share with others, and which has enriched my life and sustained me as I read his books during the loneliest two years of my life as a government medical officer in West Africa fifty years ago. None of this is so much as hinted at in the film *Shadowlands*.

After his wife died, the real C.S. Lewis wrote, under a pseudonym, an account of his sorrow—*"A Grief Observed."* The first few chapters of this book, written in the acute agony of recent bereavement, describe his feelings of abandonment by God, the door shut in his face, the echo only of his own cries thrown back at him in prayer. Some of us have lived through times of sorrow such as this. *Shadowlands* the film finishes on this note, with a bitter and bewildered man struggling to salvage the pieces of his life, his protective "shadowland" shattered by cruel reality.

Here is a great man's life concluding "not with a bang but a whimper"—no doubt an ending to give a sense of satisfaction to an agnostic film producer. The reality, however, was very different. In the later chapters of his book, Dr. Lewis finds once again that God is near and real and had been with him all along.

Having said all this, if *Shadowlands* causes even one more Christian to discover and read the work of C.S. Lewis for themselves, the film (and this review) will have been worthwhile.

Keeping Connected in a New Era

My favourite dinosaur of the Knowledge Network is a mournful creature dying on the edge of a dried-up swamp, while lightning flashes, searing hot winds blow and fires rage in the background. All this is the aftermath of a meteorite the size of two city blocks landing on the shoreline of the Yucatan Peninsula seventy million years ago, we are told. The pathetic hero of this imaginative saga has a cow-like voice which it uplifts in lament at the passing of its own life, and indeed the passing of the whole Mesozoic Era.

I can empathize with this creature and its complaint is mirrored in this article, for I, too, am seeing the passing of an era, though I have a certain hope for the future which the prehistoric victim was denied.

Old age, the time of the well-advertised Golden Years, is a time of good news and bad news. Taking the bad first, it is the time of bereavement. Loss of friends and loved ones, loss of job, health, strength, position and much, much more. I am very well aware of my many blessings, but even so there are moments in the early morning, as my arthritic orchestra starts to play a thundering protest at having to operate for yet another day, when mild depression, for a few sad moments, rules the mind. I do not remember this happening in my youth.

The cure is not long delayed, and after a quick cup of tea I find that a vision of my miserable, wasted life is no longer passing before my half-open eyes. My morning quiet time completes the recovery, and for the rest of the day, the counting of blessings leaves no time for dwelling on the bereavements. However, a newly discovered loss has recently arisen in my consciousness. I am being disconnected from my own *Christian* culture.

The evidence has been building up more or less unawares, masked by the well-accepted and familiar fact that I *should* be disconnected, in a sense, from the outlook of the unbelieving world around me. After all, the Lord is going to sever the connection completely at any moment. It is the severing of connection with the postmodern *Christian* world that has caught me by surprise.

A few weeks ago, I heard a Sudanese Christian refugee give an amazing account of the opportunities he had found for spreading the gospel among Muslims at home and overseas, using the many features of the Internet. He was speaking in terms of hundreds of contacts, with some conversions. It was a campaign I had never dreamed of after twenty years working in a Muslim country. On top of that, still barely being on speaking terms with my computer, I understood almost nothing of what he said!

The culture gap is also brought home to me by my grandchildren, as loving and close a bunch of young people as one could find anywhere. They fix my VCR and hi-fi, deal with the mysteries of my digital watch, include us in their activities as far as possible and seek our help to critique their university essays. Four of them (and three wives) play an active part in our church youth work. They communicate very well with us and share many of our prehistoric ideas as well as our Christian faith; but when they are communicating among themselves, I realize they have one foot in a Christian world quite foreign to me.

The postmodern church scene leaves me baffled—so baffled, in fact, that I am not blindly critical of it like some of my more rigid contemporaries. I am slowly learning, perhaps, not to write off what I am not familiar with. A state of suspended judgement is the best I can manage, and knock-down drag-out arguments with my grandchildren are easily avoided. Like the TV dinosaur, I am witnessing the passing of an era; the era of organ music and hymn books (replaced by drums and guitars and songs projected on to a screen), of Bible studies (replaced by "sharing"), and lifetime overseas missionary commitment (replaced by short-term work trips). The new era is seeing the introduction into the church service of elements which would have been familiar to Old Testament believers (e.g., dancing), but which cause smoke and even sparks to erupt when tried out on the senior-citizen crowd today.

The gulf between many elderly Christians and the contemporary church scene is compounded by the electronic highway (this applies to non-churched seniors, too, who like me find "progress" often very trying). A recent Evangelical Fellowship of Canada leaflet advertised a new Web site, wwchristianity.ca. It stated

> *...using the concept of a virtual house with many rooms, Canadian believers are invited to take ownership by filling the rooms with content... uniting the whole body of Christ in Canada to share the vision that we believe God has given us, to connect, inform, equip and link Christians across the nation.*

For the elderly Canadian believer, I cannot imagine anything more likely to make him or her feel disconnected, confused, illequipped and separated from other postmodern Christians across the nation.

When this condition of disconnection is first perceived, it is like waking up one morning and finding that, overnight, English has been replaced by a foreign language. A few kind people still speak to one's own generation in the mother-tongue, but one suspects they only do it out of pity.

Along with the feeling of having lost contact, there is a feeling of guilt for letting it happen. The July/August 2002 issue of *Faith Today* is devoted to articles emphasizing that a knowledge and understanding of the thinking, culture and music of young adults today is absolutely essential if they are to be kept in touch with Christ. So maybe I've let slip the only opportunity I will ever have of witnessing to them. Moreover, the feeling of an ever-widening gap between my generation and the postmodern world is compounded by the ever-increasing physical deterioration that afflicts the elderly.

Thank God, common sense is beginning to take over. Two generations ago, one's spiritual health was measured by many according to a series of negative tests; not dancing, not touching alcohol, not playing cards (though all card games, including poker, can be played with "rook" cards, which were considered OK), and not going to the cinema. Those Christians who felt differently were in for a lot of homemade anxiety. Today we have progressed beyond this nonsense, but perhaps a new set of artificial criteria are in the making. Is a Christian senior citizen's spiritual health now to be measured by how well he handles Windows 98?

Actually of course, keeping connected to the Lord and my fellow Christians still really depends more on the Holy Spirit having control of my life than on my electronic know-how. Furthermore, I can bring all my concerns to Him, including what baffles me in the world I find myself in. This brings me to the good news, as I hear a little voice within saying, "That's enough, Gran'pa, you've made your point. Now quit whining. There are things you and your prehistoric friends can do to deal with the situation. Do them and shut up!"

There is a great passage on getting connected in Ezekiel's vision of the valley of dry bones (Ezekiel Chapter 37). God causes the heap of bones to separate into groups of 206 or so each, and then connects them miraculously—not just with each other, like skeletons wired together in a museum, but with living tendons, nerves and blood vessels. Then, to Ezekiel's amazement, the dead bones begin to breathe, move and stand up! Even so, the Lord can reconnect, and keep connected, the members of His Church of all ages; not only to Himself, but to one another.

I am making a positive effort to catch up, or at least to start moving in the same direction as the postmodern church. On my desk now stands a computer monitor, to the utter astonishment of all members of my family, including myself. I have now learned how to boot it up, and have withstood the temptation to boot it out of the window. I am learning how to do something that I have so far never been able to do—that is, to write directly into the machine, instead of scribbling my notes and thoughts onto scraps of paper first. Up 'til now I have, like Winston Churchill, been unable to feed my brainwaves directly into a monster waiting impatiently to digest them. The high cost of hi-tech ($25 spent in rescuing the computer from the recycling depot) encourages me to persist, but I am still in the stage when I think the whole apparatus is dumb and it thinks I am retarded.

Secondly, the Scriptures seem to teach me that discouragement and confusion are normal at times for God's people. Indeed, they may be God's special gift to keep us closely connected to Him if we are to learn anything from the example of such giants as Moses, Elijah and Paul.

We are told that Moses wrote Psalms 90 and 91. In the first he is in a melancholic mood. The old man looks back and admits God *has* been the refuge and strength of Israel in the past. Life is tough, however, and seventy years comes and goes in a flash. (You can say that again, Moses!) From then on, it's all labour and sorrow. In the next Psalm, however, he is on top of the world, inviting us to taste and see how good the Lord is, and how He protects His people from disease, war and all kinds of fears and dangers.

Apparently, all through the ups and downs, the Lord stayed connected to His servant, who ended up living another fifty years, in robust health until the end; rather like Florence Nightingale, who began to write about her frailties and imminent departure from this life in her twenties, and went on to die in her nineties after a life of extraordinary activity.

In 1954, C.S. Lewis took up the position of Professor of Medieval and Renaissance Studies at Cambridge University, a post that had been especially created for him. In his inaugural address, he described himself as a disappearing species, namely "Old Western Man." If his audience "wanted to understand the past," he said, "specimens of old western man should be of interest to them." (*Jack* by Sayer, Crossway Books, Wheaton IL; p. 360.)

The elderly can do the same in Canada; i.e., present ourselves as specimens rather than seniors, so that we can, perhaps—without giving offense—act as advocates for the good things in the Christianity of two generations ago. Our own grandchildren are already doing this with us. Whether it is to supply information about Roger Bannister or Pele (both the soccer-player and the volcano), or the *Gilgamish Epic*, it feels good still to be useful as a resource person for a younger generation.

Meanwhile, I still miss acutely some of the old hymns, particularly those by Charles Wesley. Above all, I miss the congregational prayer, which is so often crowded out by notices, "specials" and the needs of the home church. I realize that in this complaint, my Anglican upbringing is sticking out like a sore thumb. In the traditional denominations, with all the faults that so many display, there is at least a mention made in prayer for "all sorts and conditions of men." And for "governors and all in authority over us." These formal prayers used to irk me as a boy because of their sometimes cold formality, but now we seem to concentrate on our own cancers, hip replacements and Board decisions, and let the outside world take care of itself. Surely there are enough famines, plagues, and wars in the world for Christians meeting together in the "House of Prayer" to remember corporately one or two of these items *every* Sunday.

Perhaps I have strayed from the topic. What has this to do with drums and guitars and alienation from the postmodern Christian culture? Only this; prayer takes time, doesn't depend on specially trained leaders, can and should be carried out without fanfare and hype, doesn't always evoke a warm fuzzy feeling and is in fact, a very old-fashioned element in worship. Asking around in other evangelical churches, I find the disappearance of the congregational prayer is widespread. Black-footed ferrets are not the only entity becoming extinct.

If we feel that the gigantic problems of the world "out there" are too big for us to comprehend, let alone to affect by our efforts, then those very things make them ideal subjects for prayer, just as our feelings of complete impotence in the face of them are the very attitudes in a "pray-er" that our mighty God is looking for.

Rather than begin a lament all over again, I will close by considering once more our friend, the TV dinosaur. Unlike that miserable creature, my generation has the chance to stay connected even though a new environment, postmodernism, is destroying, like a meteorite, the world we knew. We can still play out at least two roles as elderly Christians. First, there is the role of "specimens," modeling the good things of twentieth-century Christianity, and avoiding the bad! "Give me (carefully selected parts of) that old-time religion," in fact. This may involve holding much more lightly our affluence, showing our indifference to our own self-esteem and identity, less concern for our rights and more for our responsibilities, and more concern for others in the world and less for ourselves. We can continue to advocate the claims of long-term overseas missions and the importance of Bible *study* in addition to "sharing." We can continue (kindly) urging for the restoration of the occasional hymn and congregational prayer.

Meanwhile, we still have two good and strong connections. The first is with our own generation of mid-twentieth-century gray- and white-headed believers and non-believers—many of whom are not far removed from the memories of things they learned in Sunday school long ago.

The second thing—and by far the most important—is the connection our Lord and Master daily asks us to keep unbroken with Himself.

Civil Disobedience, Anyone?

Two hundred West African women sat in deafening silence as I spoke to them in the Temne language of Sierra Leone. It was a meeting held during a Christian women's annual conference. Each year there is one session dealing with health matters and this year they had invited me to be the speaker. Out of the whole group, two or three of the older leaders of the assembly scowled at me with obvious disapproval. The subject I had chosen was a taboo one for a man to hold forth on, or indeed to have any knowledge of. I was speaking about Pharonic circumcision.

A few African church leaders had begun to realize the time was ripe for a more direct confrontation between their cultural practices and the voice of Christian conscience. Deeply held tribal customs, initiation rites and secret society activities had always been the last areas to be touched as the new African convert began to live out a new lifestyle under the Holy Spirit's direction. Now, as the tide of the gospel slowly rose, lapping against the walls of pagan and Muslim society, the first signs of crumbling were beginning to show in the unyielding walls of animist life, ancestor worship, polygamy and initiation rites.

Dr. Hugh Maclure

Anthropologists were stridently warning the world that Christian witness was attempting to change world cultures, to them the unforgivable sin. They seemed to be childishly unaware that *all* religions—whether atheism, Islam, Hinduism, Buddhism, Christianity or animism—affected and shaped the cultures of the country concerned and always had.

The great majority of the women accepted what I said eagerly, many of them having suffered the after-effects of clitoridectomy themselves. Even the few older women who at first objected forgave me and, in fact, I was invited back the next year. I will never forget the chance I had at that time to speak directly to this receptive audience about whether the inner voice of a Christian should, or could, grapple with customs dating back thousands of years.

To the older women in the meeting, I suggested that if they didn't want me to know or talk about female circumcision, they should perhaps stop bringing their daughters to me in obstructed labour, or for the repair of vesico-vaginal fistulae, both of them conditions directly caused by the mutilating procedures their ritual demanded.

For most Africans, secret society rituals were of the very essence of their tribal identity. To challenge them on Christian grounds was a monstrous intrusion into an area into which "outsiders," and particularly foreign outsiders, were not admitted. Refusing to take part in the ceremonies was for them the equivalent of what refusing to burn incense and acknowledge the lordship of Caesar was to the early Church.

This whole subject of allowing the new Christian conscience to speak to us about our own culture seems to be the last stronghold of the enemy to fall, whether in Africa, England or on the American continent. Our hang-ups are perhaps mostly about our money or possessions, but new ones are developing all the time as our culture tries to squeeze us into its mould. Listening at all times to the "voice within" is a real test of spiritual maturity. I, for one, have to reprogram the computer of my conscience time and time again in the light of incoming information and the daily promptings of the Holy Spirit.

There are signs that the Christian voice is winning the battle over Pharonic circumcision, at least in West Africa, just as it has won the battle over *suttee* in India and foot-binding in China. During the thirty years since the women's meeting described above, there has been a change in Sierra Leone, and now the subject of female mutilation is out in the open and is discussed by government agencies, churches and youth camps. I recently read an article claiming this change had been brought about by the Women's Liberation Movement! The exact opposite is the truth, at least as far as Sierra Leone was concerned, where for years the only voices raised in opposition to the practice were those of missionaries and some (not all) church leaders. Only a small drop in a huge bucket, but the abolition of this cruel practice will be a great step of liberation for millions of young women on the African continent.

There are many ways in which the "voice within" produces cultural change, and many metaphors to describe the process. When the Holy Spirit of Jesus has produced the Great Change in the heart of a Christian, He becomes the voice that directs the conscience. Christ said that this change should act like salt and light in the world, just as a grain of mustard seed grows silently and unseen until fruition, or leaven secretly causes the loaf to rise. Paul used other metaphors to describe the same process; the ambassador in a foreign country, the soldier fighting a battle, or a citizen setting a good example.

Inner voices may do the groundwork slowly and secretly, but the change, when it comes in a culture, may be cataclysmic. Just as pressure builds up in the ground as two tectonic plates grind against each other for years, the earthquake when it comes is a more or less explosive event. In our lifetime we have seen this happen to communism in the Soviet Union and Romania. Those countries experienced sudden—and to most people, unexpected—changes, as the result of years of prayer in secret by faithful believers both in and outside Eastern Europe.

Historically, it is not hard to find examples of this process in operation. From the beginning, when twelve flawed and fearful men set out to preach the gospel in a hostile world, the pattern seems to have been the same. When the primary aim has been to uplift Christ, the change has usually followed eventually, though this process does not necessarily work the other way round. When changing society has been the main first objective, the inner voice of Christianity has often grown silent.

When discussing the bringing about of social change by Christians, there is a tendency to draw examples only from the past—as if the gospel-power of the "inner voice" ran out of steam at the end of the nineteenth century. Thus we refer with justifiable pride to the effects of the Reformation, the cleaning up of England with Wesley's preaching, the social reforms sparked by the evangelical revival, and the abolition of slavery because of the lonely and persistent efforts of William Wilberforce. But what of the situation today?

Evidence of the Christian conscience bringing about change is not hard to find in the so-called Third World. A Bedouin Christian (perhaps the *only* Bedoiun Christian) told us recently that there were real signs of a crack in the monolithic walls of Islam, and it was his opinion that the day might come soon when, to everyone's surprise, the whole thing could crumble and come tumbling down as did communism in the Soviet Union.

At first sight, the outlook is more discouraging nearer to home. Our universities, many of them once started as Christian learning institutions, are now powerhouses of secular materialism and post-modernism, and in the pursuit of "tolerance," wide open to every kind of New Age superstition. Tolerance, of course, extends to Christianity also, so long as it, too, is tolerant in its beliefs—a contradiction in terms, since scriptural Christianity is as intolerant as agnosticism. Canada is being systematically de-Christianized, it seems, though this should make our witness to the real nature of our faith easier to proclaim, not harder.

Our Christian magazines and pulpits are full of tales of woe, though there are actually a number of issues where the voice within is bringing change. Abortions are on the decrease and the number of hospitals and doctors who are refusing to do the operation except for real medical reasons is increasing. Legislation is being discussed, on the basis of individual human rights, to protect medical personnel from dismissal for refusing to take any part in the abortions when done for non-medical reasons—i.e., ninety-eight percent of the time. The Supreme Court has ruled against the B.C. courts in the matter of child-pornography, and Trinity Western University won a hard-fought victory over a hate-inspired ruling by the B.C. Federation of Teachers, a decision widely applauded by the public, including the Canadian Civil Liberties Union.

There are, of course, constant skirmishes, and the promise of more to come, so believers have to stay awake. It is true a public poll showed a rejection by large majority of the concept of gay "marriage," and the traditional definition of marriage has repeatedly been reaffirmed by the courts. However, the homosexual lobby makes sure these issues are not left on the back burner, and with politicians and lawyers who are truly homophobic—in that they are terrified of homosexuals and their opinions—we may expect the warfare to continue. The increasing alarm of the media whenever a traditional expression of Christian morality or belief is made is some indication of the progress we are making.

The ground has shifted somewhat, and today we are seeing the Christian position assailed from the aspect of "hate" legislation. Unable to gain the victory by direct assault, the attack is now on the Bible and the pulpit. If Bill 250 becomes law, the Bible will become an officially illegal book, and any expression of a Christian opinion on homosexuality, or any requirements by Christian institutions to exclude practicing homosexuals, will be deemed illegal. How such a law could ever be enforced in a country containing ten percent Christians (and many more who hold more or less Christian views on ethics), it is impossible to imagine. Perhaps the government is planning to build dozens of new jails to handle all the brand-new criminals.

Having said all this, and it is being said ad nauseum, there are still many bright spots in the contemporary scene for those who are trying to live in accordance with the voice within. While socially things deteriorate, in the realm of science, the Christian position is becoming more and more a reasonable choice. The new cosmic orbiting telescope is producing more and more evidence that the universe had a finite beginning, and therefore, a Beginner. More and more voices are being raised in biology to support the idea of "Intelligent Design," and therefore, an Intelligent Designer of the Universe. I believe there was never a time when Christian university students had better reasons to stand firm and obey the Spirit in their consciences.

Acknowledgement of the possibility of an Intelligent Creator, i.e., Deism, is a far cry from conversion to the gospel of salvation from sin and new life through Christ, but for an erstwhile atheist or agnostic, it is a huge step in the right direction.

It is sad that so many believers seem to be quite defeatist about the possibility of the Christian conscience exerting an increasing influence for good on society. One reason for this is an extreme dispensational view which writes off society as a completely lost cause, fit only for the fires of hell. Such a view leads to fire-truck evangelism: rescuing the occupants of the burning house, but not trying to put the fire out. This was the old attitude of evangelical missions, and we encountered it when presenting to our missions board a plan to introduce a hospital-based ministry in Sierra Leone in 1946. Some of the graybeards on the committee were certain we were about to introduce "modernism" into their theologically pure mission.

Others are overwhelmed by the slow progress of change and the weight of the opposition. I have some friends who seem to be both fearful and indignant because unbelievers despise or reject the message, or plan counterattacks. They remind me of an episode from my school days when my brother and I kept a note-book in which we wrote the "famous sayings" which our teachers at school and preachers at church delivered when under stress, which was most of the time. One day our pastor, famous for spouting non-sequiturs like a leaky hose, produced this master-piece. In connection with some event that had got him worried, he announced, "It almost seems as if the Devil is against us." This became a much-used phrase in our family for many years, and we used to debate whether he meant to put the accent on *Devil,* or *is* or *against.*

People of the Voice Within, too, should not be surprised by the strength of the opposition. Christ Himself warned us not to marvel when we share some of the hatred He endured, and He assured us that in the end, the gates of Hell would fall before the Church, and that in the new heaven and new earth, the saints would be there in uncountable numbers.

At present, however, the Devil *is* against us. What did we expect when we joined up?

The question remains, "What practical steps can we take to make our lives more audible and visible to our culture?" We can live lives of integrity and serenity to give authenticity to our profession, and teach our children to do the same. We can support the Evangelical Fellowship of Canada as it acts as the voice of Bible-believing Christians within government circles, or as our legal watchdog.

Some will have opportunity to stand for office politically, though I make this suggestion with great diffidence as, for myself, I'd rather have a root canal done than sit on a committee. We can encourage our children and grandchildren to get into journalism; a suggestion too late for me to act upon now. If we could change the media, the culture would soon follow!

Lastly—and the time for this may in Canada may be nearer than we think—we may have to stand up and take part in some act of civil disobedience. If Bill 250, already referred to, becomes law, many of the most essential aspects and manifestations of our faith may be deemed illegal. If this happens, I believe there will be a real need for hundreds of thousands of Christians across the land to unite in some obvious, flagrant and public act of civil disobedience. I find it hard to believe that the powers that be would find it possible to punish, at a minimum, ten percent of the population of Canada if there was such a deliberate and coordinated action undertaken, but there might well be a dust-up of huge proportions. Throughout church history, Christian communities all over the world have had this difficult decision to make. How far will we let the state go before we dig our heels in? Why should we in North America forever be spared what has been the experience of the rest of the worldwide church for centuries?

Revolution in Haiti

ILE La Gonave is an island in the Bay of Haiti, fifty miles west of Port-au-Prince. We were working at the only hospital on this island of 60,000 people. As 1986 came to a hot and humid close, life in Haiti was explosive. Their history had been a series of leaps out of various tyrannical frying pans into assorted oppressive fires, the last one being the reign, for twenty-eight corrupt years, of the Duvaliers, father and son. It was a country steeped in voodooism, an animistic mixture of debased Roman Catholicism inextricably mixed with African spirit worship originating in Dahomey. Corruption and power-seeking by unscrupulous leaders had given it one of the most feared police systems in the world: the *Tontons Macoutes*, or "Bogey-men."

During the time we were there the Duvalier clone, Marcos in the Philippines, grabbed all the headlines. Both presidents had wives who, like Jezebel, outdid their husbands when it came to "whoredoms and witchcraft." Their appetites for luxury were rivaled only by the most shameless of our "prosperity" theologians.

Two events precipitated the revolution in Haiti, which had been brewing for many months. The president's wife flew home from a shopping spree in Paris in a chartered jet laden with clothes, shoes, luxury goods and furs (to keep her warm in Haiti's frigid climate?) and her arrival coincided with a riot in which two schoolboys were shot dead by the police. This was promptly followed by a teacher's strike, a fuel shortage, epidemics of typhoid and meningitis, riots, a crop failure, drought and gathering opposition to the Duvalier regime. Revolutionary parties sprang up like weeds, each one threatening and beating up anyone not supporting them. It was very reminiscent of Sierra Leone before an election. We kept our heads down, minded our own business and prayed for peace and freedom from surgical emergencies at night, which would have to be operated on without adequate light (no fuel for the generator).

For many weeks we lived on the rich diet of rumours provided by Radio Haiti, the Voice of America and various visitors who came to the island from Port-au-Prince. We heard our hospital was to be looted within a few days, missions on the main island had been sacked, Cuba was invading, Port-au-Prince was in flames while its streets ran with blood. We heard the American Marines had landed and our island's food supplies were to be cut off by one of the rival political parties. Only the good old BBC reported the news with true British coolness, advising patience and a stiff upper lip until the situation clarified: It was most annoying to some of the more volatile of our colleagues. I remember being told to be sure I was in close touch at all times with the Canadian embassy— a difficult assignment, in view of the fact there was no Canadian embassy in Haiti as far as we knew. Actually, since we were in an American mission, our security was taken care of by the American embassy instead.

We continued to see a hundred or more patients a day at the hospital and struggled through surgery without proper lighting. We noticed a steady deterioration in the cases of malnutrition and increase in the frequency of trauma.

Of Course I'm Biased

At last, in February 1986, it dawned on the Duvaliers that they were not the most loved leaders in the world. They flew away by night. In the next few days, most of their ministers were intercepted trying to leave the country. Commercial flights were halted as happy mobs, celebrating their freedom, hunted down politicians hiding in the airport buildings.

With the president gone, the army declared open season on the secret police, and this time the streets of Port-au-Prince really did run with the blood of the *Tontons Macoutes*. Pretty soon, real villains having been dispatched with a machete, the slaughter turned to the elimination of personal enemies. A mob could be relied on to dismember anyone who was casually accused of having been a member of the hated secret police. Fugitives fled to the mountains and also took refuge on our island, where they survived by pillaging remote villages. Both attackers and attacked ended up in our care at the hospital.

Old grudges of all kinds were settled. Those who had profited during the swine-fever scare a few years previously had their houses burned to the ground. (Inspectors had killed pigs, but withheld the compensation provided by the American government.) The motor scooters and ghetto blasters of those who had grown rich from the drug traffic ended up in the ocean, and of course, innocent people were also caught in the crossfire. The nights were noisy with gunshots and tense with threats, but nothing stopped the patients from lining up for treatment! They came and came, hungry, fearful and perplexed, with their pulmonary TB, meningitis, cerebral malaria, typhoid, wounds and obstructed labours.

Throughout these roller-coaster weeks, the evangelical church maintained its witness, preaching mercy and forgiveness, not revenge. We heard at least four sermons on Romans 12:19. I even prepared one to give myself, in my stumbling Haitian Creole, but violence in the village to which I was to go cancelled the service at the last moment. All foreign women were advised to leave the country. My own faithful wife refused to go until our contract with the mission was up, when we could go home together.

Stripped of external aids to security, we observed Haitians exhibiting stark, primitive Christian faith, entirely dependent on the Lord for safety, sustenance and all present needs as well as future security. We came to realize that this faith was far removed from the "trusting the Lord" which well-nourished, warmly clothed, welfare-protected, adequately insured, RRSP-buffered, comparatively affluent Canadian missionaries, with their passports, exit permits and secure jobs outside Haiti, had to practice.

By the time we were due to go, the airport had reopened and things had simmered down a bit. We crossed the twelve miles of sea to the main island in a twenty-four foot sailboat. The blustery wind gave us a rough passage, but also augmented the outboard motor, so we made it in two hours. During the whole voyage, my brave little wife, who doesn't trust any vessel smaller than a B.C. ferry, kept her eyes tight shut and her head buried inside my jacket. We then made the forty-mile road trip into the city with only minor incidents. Later that day, riots broke out again and the airport was closed once more. Finally, four days later, we were able to hop a ride on the Missionary Flights International mail plane, a forty-five-year-old DC 3 which slowly rattled its drafty way the 500 miles to West Palm Beach in four hours flat.

I have a T shirt with "Haiti Libre, 1987. Vive La Liberte" on it, but after two hundred years of struggle toppling tyrants and replacing them with other tyrants, few seem to understand where true freedom comes from. At least now a growing church, totally ignored by the Canadian news media, continues to grow, spreading the news that God's Son can make a person free indeed.

The High Cost of Medical Missions

Written in 1989.

"MEDICAL Missions"—two words which, in the old days, were carefully segregated from the main missionary enterprise in the minds of evangelical "missiologists." For instance, in 1888, R.N. Cust argued that missionary money "was collected for the purpose of saving a soul, not sharpening an intellect." By 1894, he had thawed to the extent of including "a lay evangelist, a female evangelist or a medical evangelist wherever the gospel preaching is the substantive work." (*Christian Mission in the Modern World,* by John Stott, p.16, IVF.) This attitude has been referred to as "mouse-trap" or "fire-truck" evangelism, in which educational or medical service was regarded as the bait in the trap to catch converts, or as the fire-truck rescuing the victims trapped in the burning house, the fate of the house being of little if any importance.

The thinking behind this view of evangelism and missions was a reaction against the growing influence of those who claimed the gospel could only be expressed today in sociological terms; a message that is still being expressed by organizations who have abandoned the Bible as their guidebook. My wife and I ran up against the remains of this old and rigid suspicion of "social" aspects of the missionary calling when we first applied to work as medical missionaries in Sierra Leone in 1946. I'm glad to say the objections were short-lived and we received nothing but encouragement from the missionary board once we began our work.

I believe a more "holistic" view of missions is the scriptural teaching, and Jesus was very specific about the nature of the "gospel," telling and showing His disciples what the Father sent Him to do on earth (Luke 4:18,19), and then telling them to do the same (John 20,21). In other words, His acts of healing and compassion were part and parcel of the "gospel."

Though the message of medical missions is inseparable from the preaching of the good news about Christ, West Africans seem to have no trouble at all in dividing them. Western medical care is accepted with wild enthusiasm; the message of the Cross with cautious or mixed response.

First, with regard to medical work—we in West Africa are better off than our colleagues in Nepal, for instance, where most of the people viewed the coming of a Western doctor with indifference and reckoned that, as no one ever does anything except to gain merit, the doctor should be grateful to them for giving him an opportunity to pile up cookie-points in the cosmic scheme of things, as Dr Dale writes in his fascinating book, *Don't Let the Goats Eat the Loquat Trees*. What a contrast to Sierra Leone, where gratitude abounds. Half-starved patients bring long-gone catfish and athletic roosters for services rendered, or in hope they will be rendered, and sometimes for no reason at all, and even the customs officials at the airport thank us for coming and for operating on their relatives.

For all that, there are many obstacles that culture and circumstances cast in the way of "health-care delivery" as it is quaintly called nowadays. If we in the Western world still obstinately cling to lethal lifestyles, what can be said of a country loaded with ignorance and disinformation? Apart from this, education may often have surprisingly little effect on the cultural patterns of Muslims and animists, and it is so often cultural patterns that are behind the diseases.

In a West African village, blood donors are hard to find, children are scalded because cooking is usually done on the ground, mosquito nets are not available or are expensive, reading and the accumulation of knowledge is thwarted by darkness summer and winter from six-thirty on. Even in the hospital, the rural patient's skill at putting the cart before the horse is shown by the fear of nasogastric tubes (babies with tube-feeding are the sicker ones and therefore more likely to die); big spleens are thought to cause malaria, breast milk in the ears of children is thought to make them discharge, diarrhoea is feared less than constipation, blood-stained sputum causes pulmonary TB and so on ad infinitum.

Dr. Hugh Maclure

Birth control measures are thought by many, in a land without insurance and old-age security, to lead to destitution in old age, water is not boiled before drinking because firewood is scarce and getting scarcer, eggs are not given to women or children for cultural reasons, and injections are always the best medicine.

Of course, one could go on in this vein for several pages, but we must not forget that in our culture, we, too, are guilty of many medical superstitions and we have less excuse for it. However, it is the sheer multitude of popular errors in the minds of our African rural patients that makes treating them in their own setting interesting, to say the least.

Poverty is another obstacle. The hospital where we worked was one of the busiest in the whole country, but for all that, many patients simply could not afford to come at all, however sick they might be. True, we had an "indigent fund," swallowed up by the increase of TB cases at the moment, and no one *in extremis* was ever knowingly turned away for lack of money, but a trip to the hospital in itself may mean an expensive journey of days in a hammock or truck. On top of this, there is the expense of lost harvest, lodgings on the way, and soon half a year's income is gone.

As the economy plunges, there is a resurgence of "country" medical treatment, and for all the PhD theses written on indigenous medicines and healers, the overall effect as seen by the hospital is wholly appalling. This as a cost paid by the African in mothers dying undelivered, stillborn babies, women with bladders and birth canals mutilated, fractures arriving too late for anything but amputation and many children poisoned after taking "native medicine."

By contrast, preaching and church-planting has to overcome totally different obstacles. Patients are desperate to embrace Western medicine, if the circumstances allow them to do so, but with Christianity it is another story, and pagans and Muslims have their own religious agenda. However cordial the reception given to a white missionary, the African convert in a Muslim village is usually treated quite differently. He or she may scoffingly be called "White man" or "Preacher," and a Christian still dependent on his or her parents may get no food at all on Sundays if church takes the place of working on the farm ("no work, no food"). Muslim husbands will very likely lose their unconverted wives, and Christian wives, their unconverted husbands.

Of course, there is always the mass of patients who will profess conversion, or do *anything* to get a job, a meal or worm medicine. These degrade Christianity in the eyes of their culture, just as "prosperity theology" degrades it in ours. It also adds one more obstacle for the witnessing Christian to overcome.

These are some of the factors, partly due to culture and partly to ignorance, which complicate medical work, but above all slow the rate of church growth in a mixed animist and Muslim population. They particularly slow the growth in the area where it is already in difficulties, i.e., among working Africans outside the "mission." Desperately needed are *practicing* Christian farmers, policemen, truck drivers, traders, carpenters and craftsmen. We are grateful to the Lord that we now have a Christian trader as president of our African Conference, and one who lives as a light in the secular world. (Note, this man was shot to death during the civil war of 1992-2001.)

One is sometimes tempted to ask the question that our society asks all the time about a program—are medical missions cost-effective? In Muslim lands, where church growth is so slow and so remorselessly indifferent to the projections of Church Growth missiologists whose experience has been in religions other than Islam or Buddhism, we might be tempted to say "No." But of course, for the Christian, after the initial counting the cost of discipleship, cost-counting is no longer on the agenda. Obedience and grateful awe in His presence, like the grateful woman who ignored the cost when anointing the Master's feet with oil, are the attitudes Christ demands, and they alone justify the high cost, including the financial cost, of medical missions.

We have barely mentioned the high cost of scientific medicine—a cost that is bankrupting the Western world, and is simply not paid at all in most countries near or south of the equator. The entire health budget of Sierra Leone and a score of other countries cannot even cover the cost of a comprehensive inoculation program for the children who live there.

There is a high cost paid, too, by medical workers. So far at our hospital, we have not yet been able to find an African doctor willing to work in the hospital on a missionary salary, though we have a growing band of competent and dedicated nurses and technicians. The problem is present in East Africa, also though is not quite so acute there, I understand. Meanwhile, women missionaries, nurses included, pay an immense price for their devoted service. In our hospital, their day was usually longer than the doctor's, and they paid, too, in the isolation and missed chances for advancement and marriage. A nurse's work included a killing load and little chance for recreation or choice of friends.

That doctors also pay a price is obvious in that fewer and fewer are willing—except for a very short time—to come and pay it by grappling with conditions so very inadequate when judged by the standards they have been trained to regard as essential for the efficient (and legally safe!) practice of their profession. I had many a moment of terror when I first landed in Africa! Surgical, medical and obstetric horrors well beyond my experience or training, no consultants, no blood bank or hi-tech laboratory and a patient who complains in three different languages, not one of which I understood! All this quickly makes even an experienced MD feel like a trembling intern again! Add to this a bundle of keys weighing half a pound, locked rooms containing all the essential equipment and a generator to start makes a call at 3 a.m. a hair-raising experience. Medical missionary life may make you long for early retirement, except for the fact that it leaves you with nothing to retire on!

As I write this, the hospital I've been referring to needs more doctors—a few long-term and many short-term volunteers. In fact, short-term medics, paying their own way and available in steady supply, could immensely relieve the regular staff. Yet the logistics of getting there, learning the ropes and meeting the challenges are difficult and costly. No more costly financially, though, than a vacation safari to the East African game parks. Looking at my medical friends, none of them noticeably suffering too much in a depressed economy, I know many of them could afford it, and if they took the plunge, they would never be the same again.

The ABC Phenomenon

EVERY eye at the table swivelled onto me like a searchlight. I had made what I thought was an innocent remark, but the reaction it produced was as if I had just dropped in from Mars and announced there was conclusive evidence in outer space that the resurrection had never happened.

Our speaker's subject had been Creation, by which he meant "creation science." He outlined how the Lord God had made everything out of nothing by the Word of His power. He continued, pointing out that it was obvious to all those who believed the Scriptures and had not been led astray by the oppositions of science, falsely so-called, that He had done it in six days of twenty-four hours each, a few thousand years ago. He cited evidence from geology, moon dust, the earth's magnetic field and other sources to back up his thesis, and reminded us not to be surprised if unbelieving scientists scoffed at the plain teaching of the Bible.

Here was a perfect example of the **ABC** phenomenon, where **A** equals what the Bible actually says (Creation was the work and plan of the Creator, not random chance, and was described as taking place in six stages called "days"); **B** equals our interpretation and understanding of what the Bible is saying (the days were of 24 hours each and it all took place a few thousand years ago); and **C** equals what unbelievers think about both **A** and **B** (it's poetry, myth or nonsense).

But what of my timid little comment? I had said that perhaps the evidence for a planned creation rather than naturalistic evolution was considerably stronger than for the proposition that it all took place in six days of twenty-four hours each, and I felt the distinction between the two statements should be kept separate in our minds. More particularly I felt it was unfair to make the "creation science" description of things a test of Bible-believing orthodoxy.

My point, which I so dismally failed to get across, was not that my particular explanation of the first chapter of Genesis was correct (i.e., big bang about seventeen billion years ago when, in a fraction of a second, the Lord made matter, energy, time, space and the basic forces in the universe out of nothing). I simply wished to point out that **A** and **B** should not be welded too closely together in our minds.

An arctic winter descended over my end of the table while we finished the meal. The foundations of "creation science" were not to be shaken so easily. Nevertheless, I am still certain I had a valid point, and with every new advance in the sciences of biology and astrophysics (the bits I can understand, that is), I am more and more convinced of it.

We all know students, brought up to believe in one particular **B**-type interpretation of the Bible's teaching on creation, who have lost their faith in **A** when their university professors have made **B** untenable. In a day when the evidence for a Beginner and Designer of the universe is multiplying, it is more than ever a tragedy when belief in **A** fails to pass the "secular university" test.

I do not mean we can only believe Scripture if science backs it up. There is, however, a "science rightly so-called" as well as the other kind, and scientific observations and theories may be accurate even when unbelieving scientists are making them. Of course, they may also be false. My point is we should not tie our trust in the authority of the Bible too tightly to anyone's ideas of what the Bible means. When my car breaks down, I trust the science of engineering to put it right, even if the mechanic is an agnostic. I believe the Bible is in accord with that kind of science *when we interpret it correctly*, but it is dangerous to attach to **B** the same infallibility that only belongs to **A**.

The **ABC** phenomenon is seen in many other areas, one of the most thorny being eschatology. **A**-type teaching clearly states in both Old and New Testaments that the King is coming back, and the signs of the last days, i.e., the Church Age, were foretold to keep us alert and fearless in troubled times. We are also strictly forbidden to guess the exact time of His return. Yet, we all hold **B**-type beliefs about the second coming, the role of the earthly nation Israel, the rapture and the millennium. Certain editions of the Bible have footnotes of **B**-teaching which have become the touchstone of evangelical correctness in North America. Someone has put it in a nutshell:

> *My hope is built on nothing less than Scofield's notes and Moody Press.*
> *I dare not trust the sweetest names, but simply lean upon King James.*

As in the creation debate, this plays into the hands of the Enemy. When the daily news conflicts with **B**-type teaching, doubts or even cynicism about the Lord's return may result.

I am writing to unite, not to divide. The Bereans supremely followed **A**-type teaching (Acts 17:10,11). Thank God *they* did not have Bibles with footnotes!

Word for Word

FOR many years, in the humid darkness, the dreaded predators had been wreaking their havoc. Unseen by human eyes, the terrible jaws tore and shredded their prey while small creatures of the night scavenged the fragments or dragged them away to dark corners where they reared their young.

While reading these words, perhaps a mental picture comes to mind of *Tyrannosaurus rex* slavering over a victim in some dark Jurassic jungle. Actually, I am describing what went on the bottom right-hand drawer of a desk in a mission house in central Sierra Leone in the middle years of the twentieth century.

The termites, gram for gram far more destructive than a carnivorous dinosaur, had teamed up with the mice and cockroaches to destroy a rough translation of the New Testament in the Temne language; proof that it is possible to feed on the Word of God without deriving any detectable spiritual benefit from it.

The manuscript upon which the pests had feasted for so long was the labour of a missionary lady who died in 1941 with the translation uncompleted. She had, for thirty years or more, survived the health hazards of that time, which included yellow and blackwater fever, finally earning a well-deserved reputation as one of the saints of the West African church.

For twenty years, her manuscript lay waiting for a translation committee to be formed so that her work could be corrected and published. Meanwhile, the pages gradually disappeared under the onslaught of insects, rats and mice as happens so often in Africa to organic material, particularly if it is valuable.

In 1953, I was asked to form the committee that would bring the remains of the translation papers into print. I realized it would be a formidable task as soon as the brittle heap of fragments was handed over to me.

The "manuscript" consisted of a pile of fragile papers stained with mouse droppings and urine, as full of holes as a Gruyère cheese and emitting that weird smell peculiar to neglected organic material in the wetter areas of the tropics. A cockroach peered out from a hole in the title page. On closer observation, large chunks of the pastoral epistles had long ago made their contribution to the health and welfare of the termites, while the Revelation was missing altogether. The paper itself had a tendency to turn to dust and ashes at a touch, as if it was some priceless medieval document.

Thus began the process of turning the written Word of God in English into *Arim ra Kuru* in Temne. We aimed at "words for words" rather than "word for word," which in translation is neither possible nor desirable.

In England during my teens, though I was sure God was calling me to be a missionary, I very firmly intended to avoid at all costs getting involved in Scripture translation. Yet here I was, twenty years later, facing a sour-smelling heap of junk with instructions to turn it into the Temne New Testament. God's ways are not our ways.

The Temnes of north-central Sierra Leone consist of about a million people, making them the second-largest tribe in a country of three and a half million (1956). It was the first language, other than West African Krio—a variety of pidgin English—I seriously tried to learn, and by the time I was asked to be on the translation committee, I could speak and understand it perhaps as well as my committee members could speak my language. It belonged to the "semi-Bantu" group linguistically, and apart from having eight or nine "pronouns" which governed the alliterative structure of the sentence, it was without the tonal and mechanical difficulties that thwart the foreigner trying to learn and speak so many other African languages, Zulu, for instance. The greatest problem I had in using the language correctly was an inability to produce a click between my middle and ring finger when flapping my hand for emphasis, as a true Temne would do! However, as far as my mouth, lips and throat were concerned, I don't think I had too much of a problem, and as every teenager knows, a click can be produced using the thumb and middle finger. I only knew one white man, born in the country, who could make the click in the authentic way.

The history of biblical translation has been a battlefield of conflicting principles. The Temne New Testament itself had been delayed for twenty years, partly because of the debate over which word to use for "God," since, of course, every word has its own connotation—particularly African tribal religious words. The Koranko translations used the Muslim word "Allah" for God, which required a lot of explaining to the uninstructed listener or reader; but for the animist, *Kuru Masaba* was equally inadequate or misleading. In the end, we used the animist word with some misgivings.

Matters of vocabulary were the least of our problems. Do we translate proverbs literally or find some Temne equivalent? Do we manufacture words when there is no word available in the tribal language—e.g., "snow"? Temnes do this all the time as they come in contact with a foreign culture; for example, *abolat* for a foreign-type hat. Even using the Temne word for "hyena" as a substitute for "wolf" opens the door to those who claim the New Testament is an inaccurate forgery. (Ahmadiya Muslims, for instance.)

What about other religious words? "Heaven" and "hell," among others, are words Muslims are familiar with, but again their understanding of what they signify is very different from the Christian meaning. The Temnes have a tribal ceremony that, on the surface, looks much like a Christian baptism, Should we use the word for this ceremony with all its animistic connotations, or "Temnefy" the word "baptize"? Eventually that is what my African friends recommended.

How providential that Hebrew poetry does not depend on rhyme for its effect! Our own Scottish metrical psalms show us what tortured English has sometimes to be employed when rhyming is the aim of the translator.

To continue. Should we translate literally or paraphrase, i.e., do we go for word for word or meaning for meaning? (Imagine the confusion the sentence "He ate hotdogs to his heart's content" could cause if translated word for word into, say, French!) What about regional dialect differences? (The word for a good woman in the north may be the word the southerners use for a bad woman.) What about regional differences when you are trying to write phonetically? Northern members of the Limba tribe can barely understand their own language when spoken by someone from the southwest. What if the seat of honour is on the left, not the right, of the king? These are just a few of the obstacles that have to be borne in mind by all members of a translation committee, whether black or white.

Any rule made has to be adhered to throughout the translation. In 1768, a certain Rev. Harwood decided to make the translation to end all translations. Combining word for word, commentary, paraphrase and footnote all at once, he left no stone unturned to make sure his readers understood the meaning of the text. Matthew 6:7 came out like this—

> *Think not that the design of prayer is, by direct importunity, to tease the Deity into compliance with our requests. Carefully avoid therefore, the error of the heathen who think that the Supreme Being can be prevailed upon by enthusiastic clamours and constant unvaried repetitions of noisy expression.*

It seemed to our committee that Rev. Harwood's technique was to be avoided.

I once saw somewhere the phrase, *the race is not to the swift nor the battle to the strong*, as it would have been stated in a medical report:

> *Double-blind crossover studies have conclusively demonstrated that success in athletic or military endeavours is unrelated to genetically determined physical characteristics.*

Rev. Harwood would have gone down well in the Canadian Medical Journal. The Bible translator, too, has to resist the temptation to amplify.

Another example to strike fear into the heart of an expatriate translator, and one that we trusted our Temne committee colleagues to correct, was illustrated in an instruction manual which came with our new Argentinian kerosene refrigerator. Written on the guarantee were these immortal words:

> *Each equipment "Turena" is guaranteed for five years. But for the quality of his materials and the proved efficiency of his absorption system, the perfection of his functionation is practically unlimited, because by the recommended treat and care, lasts for ever.*

Even the apostle Paul, writing with holy passion to his friends in Corinth, never quite got as convoluted as that. We trusted our African colleagues—some of them powerful preachers in their own language—not to allow similar mistakes by the foreign white man on their committee.

Although "word for word" is no way in principle to translate from one language to another, it is, of course, essential when copying a document so as to pass it on to the next generation. Thank God for the nitpicking accuracy of the Massoretes, the "Keepers of the Tradition," who painstakingly copied, word for word, comma for comma, jot for jot and tittle for tittle, ultimately giving us with extreme accuracy much of our Scriptures today. Using their own system of mathematical cross-checking, and no doubt bringing on early deterioration in their long-suffering eyes, they achieved an astonishing level of reliability and accuracy.

Just how diligent they had been was revealed in the flurry of research which started after a Bedouin boy threw that famous stone into the cave in the hillside eight miles south of Jericho in 1947. Searching for a lost goat, he accidentally smashed some pottery, and in due course, a twenty-four foot scroll of Isaiah turned up—more than 1,000 years older than the previously known manuscript. Comparisons showed how amazingly accurate the copying had been over the intervening 1,100 years or so.

Verbal translating or interpreting is another matter, and here again, word for word translation is rarely appropriate. Skilled interpreters in West Africa often speak almost simultaneously with the first speaker, trading meaning for meaning, idiom for idiom, proverb for proverb, following the speaker's inflection, smoothly correcting perceived mistakes and making up an entirely original message if the speaker becomes too unintelligible. We heard one such interpreter translate the words, "Now looking at it from another point of view" as "Now he will crow from another stump," without a moment's hesitation.

When we started translating, therefore, we had to establish principles. Word for word where necessary, style for style, simplicity where the meaning was clear and using the help of other versions and commentaries where it was not. Many of Paul's sentences, with verbs missing and unfinished thoughts hanging in mid-air, had to be paraphrased. We had to remember that any translation that made crystal-clear what was uncertain in the original was probably not a correct translation!

Two things soon became clear. The first was that, because of gaps in the remaining bits of the original work as well as inconsistencies in the spelling used, we would have to re-translate the whole of it from beginning to end. The second was the quite unexpected conservatism of my committee members, who were much more inclined to resort to word for word translation of the King James version than I was. To further complicate matters, there were *some* passages where every single word in the English, let alone the original, *was* of vital significance (e.g., Galatians 3:16 and a great deal of Romans).

In the end, the translation was a compromise reached by the committee with the help of New Testaments in Limba, Mandingo, French and several modern versions and paraphrases. Obviously, without Hebrew and Greek scholars around, it was a "low-level" translation, as are so many of the Scripture translations into smaller tribal languages. Nowadays, done as it was without the help of computers and by people without formal linguistic training, it would be considered inadequate. In actual fact it served its purpose for forty-five years, and is only being revised and re-translated as of 2002.

I think if I was to do it all over again, I would have tried harder to override the committee on several of the occasions when they treated the King James version as if it was the original inspired words of God. For instance, to translate literally the words, "*Jesus opened His mouth and said unto them*" could be taken to mean He began to curse them, and "*O generation of vipers*" is meaningless as far as I can determine in Temne. "*No man can serve two masters*" might be better understood as "the goat with two masters dies of starvation" (a Haitian proverb, but I'm sure there is a Temne equivalent). We might have used the proverb "Men without children selling medicine for fertility" instead of "*Blind leaders of the blind*," and so on. Perhaps, though, we were wise to err on the conservative side. Later we translated *Pilgrim's Progress* and let our hair down a bit more!

Every two or three weeks, our committee moved to a different part of the tribe so that we could try out our translation on the local population and ensure we were using language that could be generally understood throughout the various sub-dialect areas. Wherever we went, much of our work was done under the patient stares of more or less sick people, waiting with the remorseless patience of the suffering African, and often we would be interrupted by a real emergency.

Gradually, the committee members grew bolder in correcting me, and we were saved from some of the grosser errors of translations directed by foreigners. Then came weeks of typing, the extra phonetic script characters on the typewriter successfully baffling the professional help we had hoped to get. Finally, after eighteen months proofreading in our spare time, the New Testaments came from the British and Foreign Bible Society, the parcels arriving unmolested at our village in north-central Sierra Leone.

How precarious are the lives of those who have no Word of God to celebrate! Physical life on bread alone leads to protein-calorie malnutrition, with its emaciation, pot-belly, flaky-paint rash, cottony ginger hair and whining misery. We had a ward full of such kwashiorkor kids in Uganda for a year. Similarly, in the spiritual realm, we all know what a culture is like that celebrates the words of humans to the exclusion of the Word of God. A culture that is fragile, fearful, whining and swollen with luxury in places, while wasting away in others.

So, we celebrate the words of man with caution and misgiving. The Haitians, who chant slowly and mournfully in French sing with great gusto in Haitian Creole. A popular and cynical secular song celebrates the emptiness of human words in a culture ruled by Voodooism—

> *The world is very wicked and Satan works overtime,*
> *So you'd better watch out.*
> *If you put your confidence in man you'll be disappointed.*

This little bit of world-weary wisdom reflects the words of the Lord in Jeremiah 17:5-7. But in the Bible, the Word of the Lord did not stop at verse five. We celebrate the living Lord who provides the remedy in verse seven;

> *Blessed is the man who trusts in the* LORD,
> *Whose confidence is in him* (NIV).

Being allowed to use the words of men to spread the Word of God so that it might become the word for all mankind parallels the incarnation. Just as God in humility and submission became man, even so, in translation, the Word of God submits to the indignity of being confined in human words. It is not so in Islam. In our experience, Muslims were not at all eager to have the language of Allah (Arabic) translated into the language of infidels.

It is all part of that wonderful process in which the unthinkable and indescribable is spoken and written about in the understandable terms of human experience. We abide in Christ as if He was a house, we rest in Him as if He was a mattress, we praise Him as if He was Pavarotti. We describe Him in human family terms. He invites us to do so and we have no other way in which to communicate or understand invisible spiritual reality.

The life-giving Word becomes English or Temne or Lugbara for life-needing people, and in the process of becoming human words, there is a humiliation, just as in the other Incarnation. The everlasting Word becomes marks on a paper, vulnerable to the ravages of time, termites and vermin, and subject to the whims of human unreliability, yet always ultimately protected by the Holy Spirit. And so the Word becomes written, embedded in human hearts and minds, a priceless treasure which neither moths nor rust—nor termites—can corrupt.

Believe in Small Groups

"IT *is not good for man to dwell alone.*" Bible statements are sometimes true even when quoted out of context. Christians and others need to associate at times in small groups. It is a built-in law of nature, like gravity or $E=MC^2$. One could even argue that most (though not all) of our disappearing species are of lonely habits. The sociable chimpanzee fares better than the solitary orangutan!

There are far more compelling reasons, however, for Christians to join small groups. First, our Instruction Manual tells us to associate together for prayer (Matthew 18:20), witness (Acts 4:31) worship (Hebrews 10:21–35), Bible study (Colossians 3:16), fellowship (Malachi 3:16) and for many other reasons and absence of reasons. After all, our Triune God is, in Himself, a Small Group.

Second, almost every aspect of life shows us the advantages of group action. For myself, my life has been a succession of small group activities. Starting, of course, with my family, I moved on to Christian small groups at school and university, then medical refresher groups both Christian and secular, Bible study groups, men's groups, seniors' groups, prayer groups, groups for athletic events such as soccer, skiing and cycling, camping, singing, New Testament translation, artwork, writing and the list goes on and on. Finally, for sixty-two years of my life, that smallest and most intimate small group consisting of man and wife has been my strength and joy.

The small groups my wife and I have been in for Bible study, prayer, support and fellowship have been particularly memorable. In Drayton Valley, Alberta, where we were introduced to Canadian life and medical practice, we started a home Bible study that seemed to spark a movement among the churches there, so that by the time we left thirteen years later, there were nine or ten other study groups in the town. When we moved into B.C., much the same thing happened. My wife started a ladies' group which included several Roman Catholic friends, considerably enlivening the discussion at times.

Most of my friendships have arisen from small groups and nearly all the Bible study notes and material I have amassed through the years is there because of small groups. When our third son died in Vancouver at the age of forty-five, the support and comfort of small group members was something we will always remember with gratitude.

On moving to Edmonton in our mid-seventies, we were warned we would never be able to make new friends at that advanced age, particularly in a city. Small groups soon took care of that little problem. Now that we are in an apartment, getting to know people is harder—we mostly see each other for a few seconds at a time in the elevator before scuttling back into our burrows like gophers. At first we found this situation frustrating and started going to the Tuesday morning coffee group, even though neither of us like coffee much. What a difference it made! We found ourselves in a new and friendly small group—and we didn't even *have* to drink the coffee!

Of Course I'm Biased

When first attending a new church (or school or job), a feeling of isolation is reinforced by the sight of everyone else in clusters and groups all laughing, talking and obviously knowing each other. For some, this feeling of being excluded can persist for years, whereas taking the plunge and joining a small group will dispel it very quickly, unless one persistently refuses to accept the friendship of people to whom one has not been formally introduced! (Some of my fellow countrymen have been known to have that attitude.)

To sum up: Jesus taught mainly in small groups, and sent His disciples out in small groups also. Paul became part of a small group wherever he went. Would it not have been great to be in a group that included Aquila and Priscilla, Aristarchus, Epaphroditus, Onesimus, Barnabas, Dorcas and company?

Small groups have encouraged me when down, corrected me when wrong, comforted me when sad, strengthened me when weak and loved me when I didn't deserve it. I believe in small groups!

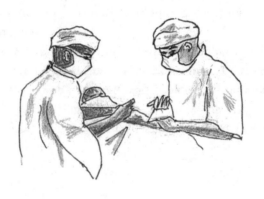

$\mathcal{M}$edical Missions: Dilemmas and Delights

ON August 10, 1984, our plane from Miami touched down safely in Port-au-Prince in a blustery crosswind, to the accompaniment of rousing applause from the largely Haitian passengers. Thus began a ninety-day work trip which took us from the crowded TB clinics of Ti Guave in the south to the nine-hour general clinics up the coast road and over the mountains to Port Margot in the north. Most of our time, however, was spent at the Wesleyan hospital on Ile la Gonave, assisting the doctors there and giving one of them a chance to take some leave. The island was the home of 60,000 or more people and the only hospital there was busy. We reached it by crossing twelve miles of open sea in a twenty-four foot boat with a heavy canvas sail and fifteen h.p. outboard motor. Fortunately the wind and the motor did not both fail us at the same time on that first visit to Haiti. (They did on a subsequent visit the following year, but that is another story!)

There have been innumerable accounts of a missionary doctor's experiences in a Third World hospital—I've written a few myself—and these are probably more fun to write than for the non-medical readers of missionary magazines to read. This article, therefore, is not about weird medical conditions or gory surgery done in grass-roofed shacks, but about some of the deeper issues of medical missions. I hope I will not lapse into the turgid language of a professional "missiologist" (abominable word!). These issues can be divided into *Dilemmas and Delights*.

1. Dilemmas

Some of those most commonly found in mission hospitals were not problems in Haiti. The hospital faucets usually delivered water, not dead cockroaches, when turned on, and stopped doing so when turned off. The X-ray machine had repair instructions in French, not Japanese (as our hospital in West Africa did), and took films of readable quality, and the generator only failed once in ninety days and never during surgery. The operating room was well equipped with all I could use and much that I couldn't, and the hospital ran smoothly with locally trained staff of a standard well above the average, we thought. Our pathology lab was adequate, and best of all, one of the other doctors actually enjoyed doing pathology!

As for the hospital in general, goats and chickens were successfully banished from the wards at all times, and dogs from the outpatient clinics on many occasions. My wife did her stuff in the pharmacy and storeroom without having to choke back screams at regular intervals as she bravely held a rat or mouse at bay, which were all in the days' work in Sierra Leone. For the comparatively smooth working of the hospital, immense credit must go to the Haitian staff, and particularly to the senior doctor—an American lady of long experience, whose formidable exterior I found somewhat intimidating at first though I soon realized she had a heart of gold as well as pediatric skills of a high order.

Short-term doctors who come to fill in, of course, do not usually get exposed to the hidden problems unless they are left alone to replace a regular doctor. After twenty years on and off, I have found, though, that certain issues are becoming more and more serious, though not perhaps obvious at first sight. They can be stated as a choice of alternatives:

A) Church Growth principles or Christian compassion?

A real conflict can develop if the principles proper to church growth in a poor country are applied too strictly to a medical program. To begin with, the first calls us to concentrate on an area of greatest response, while the second calls for action in an area of greatest need. These two principles are nearly always in conflict. For instance, it is extremely hard to apply the standard "church growth" principles to church planting among Muslims. In fact, the original "church growth" theories were first worked out and promoted by missionaries whose experience had been in South America, where Muslims were few and far between. As far as I can see, a strict application of their principles would result in complete neglect of the Muslim world. On the other hand, medical missions have proved one of the most successful ways of reaching the captives of Islam.

Perhaps all this is just the natural tension in trying to be as wise as serpents and harmless as doves. In Haiti, church growth principles might suggest we concentrate on evangelizing the cities. Medical missions, though, are most needed in the rural areas, hence our presence on Ile La Gonave.

B) Expensive Western-style medicine or what the people can afford?

A similar choice has to be made between the alternatives—treatment or prevention? Medical plans in our own country are going bankrupt over these issues. How can Third World countries avoid them? I believe there will have to be continuing and increasing subsidizing of the medical costs of mission hospitals and dispensaries overseas if we are to meet the needs of the people we are serving.

C) *Sharing our affluent resources or encouraging independence?*

This is the tension between being obedient to James 2:15,16 and not hindering the development of responsibility in the churches where we are missionaries.The goal of planting self-supporting, self-governing and self-propagating indigenous churches runs into many roadblocks. When we live in a country like Haiti or Sierra Leone, both of them near the bottom of the economic heap, we cannot help showing our affluence even when trying to show it as little as possible. If this is a conundrum in missionary work in general, it is even more so for medical missions, where one has to use highly expensive and "foreign" equipment in order to do safely what modern treatment (and the local population) requires.

One attempt to resolve this dilemma has given impetus to the modern emphasis on preventative medicine, "grassroots" clinics and the training of local women as midwives for normal deliveries. How many times have I been told that it is better to prevent a fire than treat burn cases, or that it is more cost effective to spend time treating a baby with dysentery than to be operating! In the meantime, though, that woman with an ectopic pregnancy is going to die if you don't do something expensive! The fact of the matter is that we must do both. It is little comfort to someone with a case of strangulated hernia to be told we won't treat him, but his village is being provided with a health worker who will prevent his children from catching the measles. As the hernia case knows very well that the missionary has the equipment and expertise to save his life by operating, he naturally feels that the mission won't help him because of a lack of loving care. At the same time, he is told on Sunday that Christ gave His very life to help needy and sinful people.

In practice, we do try to provide both kinds of help. Under-fives clinics, leprosy care and rehabilitation, TB clinics, rural dispensaries and the training of village health and maternity helpers, vaccination programs and nutritional instruction classes are all part of the medical program. But the problem remains. Modern treatment at the hospital level needs a constant infusion of outside money to survive in a poor country, and missionary-sending agencies are constantly short of cash! Meanwhile, people continue to be bitten by snakes and gored by wild animals, tumours continue to grow, teeth continue to ache, babies continue to develop meningitis and cerebral malaria, and women continue to be brought in after three or four days of obstructed labour.

Dr. Hugh Maclure

All the mission hospitals we have worked in have made an attempt to be self-supporting, and the patients pay as much as they can for their medicine or treatment. An increasing demand for subsidy is met to a certain extent by an "indigent" fund financed by gifts from abroad, and every foreign missionary within sight supports this fund, more or less, as well. In Africa, patients from two day's journey away, members of a tribe whose obscure language we had had the chance to learn, would struggle to the hospital and proudly present themselves to my wife and I, expecting us to be overjoyed to see such old friends. After their surgical or medical treatment and stay in the hospital or town, they would invariably have run out of money so that they could neither pay their hospital bill nor find the fare to return on the truck which would take them at least to within forty miles of their remote village. A delegation of these Koranko patients would *always* come up to our house to "greet" on these occasions; we learned to keep an indigenous fund of our own, reserved for Koranko tribespeople who otherwise would be stranded 170 miles from home without food or lodging. They seemed to calculate exactly how much it would cost to travel to the hospital. After that, it was up to Allah (and the doctor) to get them home again.

As prices increase and the economy fails, the poor are increasingly turning back to native medicine, while the hospital treats a higher and higher proportion of the richer people in the area. The people who need us most are beginning to miss out.

There are many other minor dilemmas. Do we treat the outpatients strictly in the order they register, or take those who wail loudest first, or the one who came up to the house the night before with a stringy rooster as a gift?. To act as far as possible in harmony with their culture is harder than it might appear. Ignoring the one who has brought a gift would be a deadly insult, or to make a village headman wait while a less important patient was seen would certainly not be in accord with the local customs. Some of our nurses were very strict about taking people in order as they turned up, which is certainly correct in our world, but I occasionally would make an exception for a chief or someone obviously very ill (and have been scolded by a nurse for it!). This is where triage by another member of the staff can be so useful. It enabled us to see the seriously sick without them getting lost for too long in the crowd, and it helped preserve the doctor's reputation for impartiality.

Then there is the dilemma of misunderstanding. Is conversion merely a new form of treatment? This touches the heart of an animist culture, where "sin" is something that the incomprehensible powers that be cause you to do, and illness, too, is the result of unknown outside influences. Conversion to Christ may be regarded as just one more attempt to propitiate, hoodwink, silence or persuade the powers that be. In other words, professing to "accept" Christ (a term that appears nowhere in the Bible, as far as I can find out) may have no more significance than the charm tied around the patient's ankle on first arrival at the hospital.

Similarly, to "converté" in Haiti does not necessarily involve repentance and confession of sin. The whole context of sickness and treatment adds greatly to the danger of conversion for convenience.

Now for the *delights*. There is first the delight of the sense of doing the will of God. Real issues are seen more clearly when one is away from the distractions of TV, the whining of labour leaders and the temptations of affluence. For a doctor in a mission hospital, this feeling of being in the place God wants you to be, as well as a place were you are desperately needed, is very strong. In a poor country, one rarely gets the sensation I frequently get in Canada—that one's patients are being over-doctored.

Then there is the delight of communicating the gospel in a foreign language. I have always felt that of all people, doctors and nurses have the best possible opportunity to learn a foreign language. An outpatient clinic is a perfect language school, where the same questions are asked, over and over again, with a fairly restricted range of answers, and the interpreter can be used for assistance as much or little as is required and eventually retired, whereupon female patients begin to give one an entirely different set of symptoms when no third party is present! In Haiti, even my matric French from half a century ago came in useful as a basis for picking up Haitian Creole. It was a pleasant change there to have only one language in the clinic instead of seven or eight, as in Sierra Leone.

All missionaries have the delight of making new friends each time they go abroad, a delight not restricted to the medical team.

Finally, there is the delight of learning new techniques and revising old skills not required (or allowed) to the general practitioner in Canada. No wonder elderly missionaries return again and again to the lands and people they have loved in the past.

A Piece of Cake

From Physician Magazine, March-April '02.

"I have good news and bad news for you," said the cardio-vascular surgeon, with a smile on his face like a lion contemplating an antelope with a limp. "Your renal arteries appear to be intact, but the CT scan shows a huge aortic aneurysm. You must be admitted *now*. I'll operate in a day or two."

This information enlivened our sixtieth wedding anniversary. Three weeks before the scan, a routine check-up found the bomb ticking in my abdomen, and later that evening my mind buzzed with a variety of thoughts. Memories of a long and wonderful marriage and thanks to God for His protecting hand in England, Canada, Uganda, Sierra Leone and Haiti, mingled with the awareness of the explosive waiting to detonate inside me—and the recollection of the only previous abdominal aortic aneurysm I had ever assisted on at the University Hospital in Edmonton, where the patient died on the table.

In the Maclure family there is an assortment of dentists, X-ray and ultrasound technicians and nurses, and the whole clan came round for an anniversary celebration at our house that evening. The announcement of my little problem evoked a lighter-hearted response than I had expected. They began to tell anecdotes of the "Aneurysms-I-Have-Known" type, and I was reminded that the practice of surgery had made a few advances since the Jurassic age when I practiced. I was given the impression that an AAA repair nowadays was comparable to the excision of a sebaceous cyst—a piece of cake, in fact. Even taken with a grain of salt, they were immensely reassuring.

The operation went off smoothly, and with the benefit of good analgesia I had very little pain, though I cannot now remember much of the first two post-operation days. A temporary heart irregularity was soon brought under control. Now fitted with a new Gore-Tex aorta (a synthetic tube resembling a pair of leotards for a tiny dachshund), I am back to peddling fifty miles a week on my bike. It is time to look back on the experience and see what I have learned from it.

1. Trouble is the only test of faith

My feelings of closeness to God operate like the gears on our Land Rover in Africa. Normal gear for the flat bits, and four-wheel drive for the swamps and rocky hills and when pulling an overloaded luggage trailer. When trouble comes, I find extra strength and power is available from the Lord when I downshift to "4WD" faith. When the road of life is easier again, I shift up and continue with a normal mode of trust once more, walking (partly) by sight and not relying wholly on faith in things unseen. I can thankfully say that this less-than-healthy spiritual lifestyle is gradually fading, but it is still a bad habit that I find hard to break until the next test comes along. As in Africa, I do not always "feel" assured that I'll get through the next roadblock, but in spite of the imperfections of my faith, when I come to it, the Lord provides me with the extra low gear and the hazard is surmounted. He gives us our *daily* bread.

My wife and I were in Uganda when Idi Amin propelled himself up the promotion ladder from Sergeant to Field-Marshal overnight. Six months later we were in Sierra Leone, and we addressed a conference of pastors and teachers, telling them what was happening to their fellow Christians in Uganda. They had a real fear that if troubles like that came to *their* country, they might not be able to stand firm for Christ. As their own proverb says, "*When the chicken sees the partridge getting plucked, she trembles.*" Afterwards some of them prayed that they would have the strength to stand firm if such things ever happened in their country.

Twenty years later, a ten-year civil war *did* break out in Sierra Leone, causing unimaginable havoc and destruction. I knew some of the pastors who were killed (though the violence was not particularly directed at the Christian church), and several of our friends were mutilated, having limbs cut off, or lost their homes, farms, family and often life itself. The war is over now, and looking back we hear of many areas where the church has stood firm or gained ground, and of new churches being planted.

2. Witness is most effective when faith is being tested

In Sierra Leone, they say, "Don't buy medicine for fertility until the seller has shown you his own children." And so our testimony of calmness and assurance under fire was crucial during my stay in hospital before the staff, and the family and friends as they visited.

I am at an age when I can expect great tests any day now. Both my wife and I are fifteen years over warranty, according to Psalm 90:10. Unimaginable grief lies ahead for one of us as well as illness and perhaps prolonged disability before death. Will we be able to bear this? Our heads and hearts say "No," but our Lord says "Yes!"

In Haiti, during the revolution of 1987, we saw Christians witnessing under extreme stress. Our own peace of mind and faith were buttressed by Canadian passports, return tickets, pensions, savings, investments and the like. *They* had nothing but the Lord who had delivered them from Voodooism. Would we have had the same kind of steadfast courage under the same conditions? Is there a western missionary anywhere who has never had thoughts like these?

3. A crisis enables us better to understand others' troubles.

The apostle Paul remarks on this in 2 Corinthians 1:3,4—a lesson I particularly needed to learn. I realize that my long and very happy, not to say hilarious, marriage makes it nearly impossible for me to understand or even counsel those whose marriages are breaking up. For this reason, every healthy eighty-plus-year-old doctor who has so far dodged the bullets that have laid his peers low, needs at least one life-threatening illness.

Summing up, in the words of puritan Thomas Brooks,

> *"My grace," saith God, "shall be yours to pardon you, and my power shall be yours to protect you, and my wisdom shall be yours to direct you, and my goodness shall be yours to relieve you, and my mercy shall be yours to supply you, and my glory shall be yours to crown you."*

Who could ask for anything more?

$\mathcal{E}$mpty House

IN his book, *The God Who Is There* (Hodder and Stoughton, 1968), Francis Schaeffer points out the intrinsic contradiction that lies coiled like a maggot in the heart of secular humanism, and all its manifestations. In his thirty-year-old books, Schaeffer shows us how this little worm got there and its effect on modern art, music, philosophy, culture, theology and us ever since. C.S. Lewis, too, has written much on the same subject, but more lucidly. As I watch my grandchildren trundle off to university and high school, I pray that they may have their eyes open wide enough to see this little beast.

TV provides a perfect vantage point for maggot watching, and David Suzuki is one of the clearest examples of a "naturalist," i.e., one who ignores the built-in contradictions of his own mechanistic evolutionary philosophy.

We are filled with wonder not only at the marvels of complex beauty evident in the world of natural history, so graphically shown in some of Dr. Suzuki's films, but also at the mindset that

a) explains it all in terms of a mechanistic irrational evolutionary process, and

b) exempts his own thought processes from this mindless universe.

He begs us to believe his ideas are true, while demolishing the basis of believing in the very existence of "truth" itself. If thought and human conclusions—both Suzuki's and mine—are merely an end result of irrational chemical and electrical reactions in our brains, what right has he (or have I) to believe they are true in any real sense? All we can logically say about our thoughts and conclusions is that they happen, or at least, we have the sensation they are happening, like the eruption of Mt. St. Helens, or my liking for clam chowder.

This chain of thought removes the argument (for the time being) from whether or not the theory of mechanistic evolution actually happened to whether or not *anything* has actually happened. Perhaps it is all just an effect or side-effect of the electrochemical fireworks inside my skull. If I really have a skull. It certainly removes all rational validity from the question, "are Dr Suzuki's arguments any more sensible than those of the president of an oil company?" Both parties are equally at the mercy of irrational evolutionary forces, since both are just part of nature, as Suzuki never tires of telling us.

Of course, Dr Suzuki is smart enough to spot the maggot himself, and so, going outside his own closed system without telling us, takes refuge in irrational Indian "spirituality" and the Gaya or Earth-Mother cult. Others go to different kinds of pantheism. Schaeffer's thesis is that they should go to the God Who Is There of the Bible, who has made a real world that can be rationally investigated and discussed. A world where valid moral and ethical judgements can be made. But, alas, what could be more politically incorrect?

It is a pity that, although he was no doubt a clear thinker, clear writing did not easily trickle out of Dr. Schaeffer's typewriter, because what he says is vitally important for us in this country to understand. He describes the change in basic ideas about "truth" and "non-truth" which resulted from Hegel's philosophy. Hegel replaced the "truth-untruth" (or "thesis-antithesis") formula with the concept of "thesis-antithesis-synthesis," thus blurring the distinction between truth and its opposite. Hence the modern climate of "tolerance," subjectivism and "truth-for-me."

So, behind Hegel we find our old friend, the maggot: the assumption, reached by faith alone, that our thoughts are solely produced by irrational causes. That being so, our moral and value judgements are not related to anything *real* in the universe. (Is the universe real?)

Anyone swallowing this enormous assumption suddenly finds him- or her-self like a child in a house at night with no parents. Mom and Dad, instead of being out for a show somewhere, are *dead.* They have to rely on a babysitter, either a very old and ugly woman called Mrs. Pan Theism, or her sister, younger but equally ugly Ms. New Age. They tell the kids that their parents are dead, but not to worry, they are still present in the moonbeams, in the song of the nightingale and in the sparkling stars, which just happen to be behind the clouds at the moment. The bereaved children find all this far from comforting for some reason. (We have experienced this well-meaning comfort from New Age friends when our son died.)

Writing as one who has experienced life both before and after the change in popular philosophy, which Schaeffer says seeped down to USA in the mid-1930s, I realize my grandchildren have a very different kind of war to fight in the University of Alberta than I had in London University in 1936.

Schaeffer's solution is for modern Christians to be aware of the situation, to engage where necessary in pre-evangelism (i.e., clearing away misconceptions) and to be hard-nosed about what we *know.* We believe in the God Who Is There, who is revealed truthfully in the Bible, who created a real heaven and earth with a real natural law. He is both rational and historical. He was incarnate in Jesus Christ.

Of course, pre-evangelism is another story.

The Cat's Birthday

In the 1960s, some doctors still made house calls, and many of the ones I made stick in the memory. On Galiano Island, I was called one night to a tent in the cedar forest where a young "hippie" midwife was attending her friend in labour. Neither of them really wanted an interfering Anglo-Saxon, chauvinistic male, capitalistic "scientific" doctor to have any part in the procedure, but they were willing to hear my opinion, since the labour appeared to be taking a rather long time. I humbly asked if I would be allowed to examine the mother, or did they want me to divine the problem from outside the tent? After some discussion it was decided that I could have a look and see what I thought about the progress, as long as I promised not to actually deliver the baby. I think they thought I was about to anesthetize the mother on the spot and then drag the baby out with forceps.

I found the mother to be fully dilated but the occiput of the baby's head was to the back instead of the front of the mother. The child was quite small and it was easy to turn the little head into a better position. I then tactfully withdrew, saying that I thought the birth would take place within a few minutes, but if they didn't mind, I'd stick around for a bit longer if I wasn't in the way! This they graciously agreed to, and as I made my way to a corner of the wigwam, I heard a yell from the mother, followed immediately by a tiny cry from the newborn.

Having apparently gained the confidence of these nature children, I became quite friendly with them and hopefully was able to dispel some of the misconceptions they had about modern medicine.

On another occasion, the call was to the house of an old patient, one of the town's many alcoholics, with a chronic heart condition. When I arrived he was somewhat mellow from the liquid diet he had been absorbing, but complaining of angina. His first words to me as I entered the house were, "Get your knife out doc! I need a new heart transplanted right now." I pointed out the disadvantages of this plan, not least being the fact he would be unlikely to appreciate being the guinea pig on whom I did my first heart transplant. Then I said, on the spur of the moment, "But I agree you need, like all of us, a new heart. Jesus Christ has given me a new one and He'll give you one, too, if you ask Him in repentance and faith." The patient sat up in bed and shouted "Why the hell didn't you tell me that before?" It was a sad commentary on the feebleness of my witness to him in the past.

Of course, there were many opportunities to share my faith—some, but not all, with a happy outcome. One day I stayed after the clinic was over and talked to a Jehovah's Witness for an hour. He was full of guilt and longed to have assurance of forgiveness and certainty of eternal life. I went home feeling quite proud of myself for my zeal in spreading the knowledge of the gospel. Early the next morning, my patient's neighbour called me to say he'd found him lying under a swamp poplar on his farm, with a gun in his hand and a .22 bullet in his head.

Of Course I'm Biased

Not all those to whom I spoke about the Lord committed suicide. One young unmarried lady demanded a prescription for contraceptive pills. I spent some time discussing other lifestyles with her, and in the end, she stormed out to see one of the other doctors in town. Many years later, in the Okanagan Valley, I was attending a service at the evangelical chapel and she came up to me. I did not recognize her, but she reminded me of my narrow-minded and judgemental attitude, thanking me for it. She had gone home in rage and began to think seriously for the first time in her life about "sin, righteousness and judgement." To cut a long story short, she had eventually become a Christian.

Perhaps the most memorable house call I made was in response to a frantic message from our operating-room nurse. Like most doctors, I viewed calls from nurses and doctors' wives with grave suspicion, since it is a well-known fact that their deliveries are always complicated, their symptoms inexplicable and their headaches unresponsive to treatment. However, this call was short and to the point: "Please, Doctor, come!" I could hear muffled sobbing in the background.

In this nurse's family there were two young daughters who were the owners of a much-loved cat. It was her birthday and while the cake was being prepared, this creature had, cat-like, been seeking her own comfort and found the thirty-below-zero temperature outside the house not to her liking. She climbed up under the hood of the husband's pickup truck and settled herself gratefully on the motor, which was still warm. The owner then got a call to go out. He started the engine and, on hearing an ear-piercing screech, killed the motor just in time to avoid killing the cat. When I got to the house, I saw what looked like two cats on the kitchen table. One was naked, and beside it was a blood-stained bundle of fur. Actually, the fan of the truck had nearly skinned the pet.

Dr. Hugh Maclure

I sutured the fur back on again (it was still attached in places), and the patient began to purr and drink her milk. The cake was brought out and the party proceeded as planned. When I left, puss was curled up in the best armchair with that smug expression on her face that cats wear when they know they still have eight lives left.

The moral is, keep your fanny away from the fan.

An Easter Weekend in Sierra Leone

I have been trekking with another missionary and we are spending Easter weekend in a little town ten miles north of Magbe up the Merki River Valley. This is in the foothills of the Yara mountains, one of the most remote areas of this little country. Here, many rare and disappearing species still exist and even, in some cases, abound. The only West African Buffalo I've ever seen was in this region, and sometimes one sees the skull and antlers of a bongo hanging up outside a hunter's house. We hear the hooting yell of red and black colobus monkeys and often see them two hundred feet above us in the jungle trees. Chimpanzees are common here. All these and other species are vigorously hunted by the Mansa tribesmen. The colobus monkeys are eaten wherever Islam's sway is not too strictly observed, and their long furry coats trim the skin prayer mats they use and sell to unwary strangers. As for the poor chimpanzee, it is hunted both for food, to protect the crops from its appetite, and for native "medicine," i.e., as a charm to ward off evil spirits or a miracle cure for "river blindness" (caused by a parasite, *onchocerca volvulus*). As far as eating these exotic dishes is concerned, I prefer wild cat to colobus, and baboon to either of them. In any case, when smothered in red peppers and palm-oil, who can tell puff-adder from porcupine?

From our house in Magbe we often heard the chimpanzees calling in the trees down by the river, and our boys went far in learning their language as they beat their little chests and hooted back at them!

After a three-hour walk over a rocky path, with the roots of the great trees and the frequent mountain streams making the use of a bike impossible, we reached a small town rejoicing under the name of Bandakarifaya. Speaking of bikes, I used to take one occasionally on these journeys, but soon found that the grasses and little bushes obscuring the path, which was made by Africans who always walk single file, soon formed a tangled net in and around the rear ten speed de-railer, and one ended up carrying thirty pounds of bicycle instead of riding it.

An African trader generously put us up in his house and we set up our camp beds and mosquito nets in a room about eight feet square, sharing the space with the chickens and lizards. Seventy patients immediately condensed out of the atmosphere and sat on the verandah, quietly conversing in Mansa, an activity which sounded like the start of World War III. Others peered in through the foot-square window, reducing what little visibility there had been to zero. It was all quite frustrating at times, but a frustration I often yearn to experience again now!

We walked down to the stream to bathe, talking loudly as we went, as custom demanded, to warn any bathing ladies of our approach. (There is a sensitive grass in this country which curls up when touched; the Africans call it the "Woman-cover-your-self" grass.) Then we went to see the town headman to arrange a time for a clinic, and later a service to celebrate the fact the "Nabi Yesu" had risen from the dead, and this was the day Christians celebrated the fact. We were told that both meetings were exactly what the whole town had been eagerly waiting for with bated breath. Mansas can be overwhelming in their welcome to a doctor. As for the actual fulfillment of the promised enthusiastic response, the Mansa proverb applies; *Fo a mara un nya la*— "Unless I actually see it with my eyes!"

Most of the initial crowd reluctantly dispersed, but showed up again at clinic time, the headman and his cronies bringing wooden chairs so that they could stay all afternoon and see the entertainment. Who needs TV when you can watch dental extractions or terrified infants getting injections?

In the background, two donkeys maintained a mournful accompaniment, braying sadly at regular intervals. These were "holy" creatures kept as "lucky charms" to bring good fortune to the village, and much more that the ignorant white man doesn't know about. Mixtures of Islamic and animist practices may seem harmless and even comical to us, and we believe in the God who created laughter and gave a sense of humour to us as one of His many gifts. Furthermore, secular anthropologists are adamant that we must not monkey with these tribal cultural beliefs; but the Bible is absolutely uncompromising in its insistence that the mixing of religions—particularly when Christianity is part of the mix—is an abomination in God's sight. Meanwhile, the holy donkeys caused mild havoc in the towns where they were kept, feeding in the plantations and eating clothes hung out to dry for dessert. No one dared drive them away.

The "church" here consisted of about half a dozen young men, one or two women and swarms of children. When a missionary was in the village, a rare event, several of the headmen and elders also attended out of courtesy. (The same courtesy that makes it so hard for a foreigner to know what's really going on!) Perhaps some of those who came to the service really believed, but most were cautious observers who, for the time being, were not about to forsake ancestor worship or a mixture of fetish worship and Islam.

We preached three times that weekend, meeting on the trader's verandah and proclaiming the rising of Jesus from the dead. The elders who came, squatting on their little wooden stools, included the owner of the donkeys who continued to hee-haw dolefully in the background. Almost in unison with the donkeys, the older men nodded their heads at regular intervals and grunted "Namu! Namu!" (i.e., "Right on! You can say that again! Exactly!"). Some of the young men stayed on afterwards and we talked with them about their problems and witness in this apparently discouraging environment. Out of such unlikely beginnings has sprung the Church of Christ in this and other tribes.

This short account of an Easter weekend thirty years ago evokes many memories of sights, sounds and smells, few of which relate to Canada. Yet, the Easter message is the very core of the gospel the world over. It must always be an essential part of any evangelizing or church-planting effort. Almost without exception, it was the subject of every sermon or defence of the gospel recorded in the Acts of the Apostles, whether spoken by Peter, Paul or Stephen. "If Christ be not risen," our entire message, lifestyle profession and hope for the future are all complete nonsense, and the sooner our culture buries us, the better.

Once, in Enderby, a university student from UBC asked me why Christians made such a fuss about a man who lived two thousand years ago (if the records were reliable, which he doubted). I replied that he (the student) would make a fuss, too, if he really believed that Jesus Christ's rising from the dead was the same sort of historical event as the French Revolution or the Battle of Stalingrad. His reply was, "Oh well, yes, I sure would!"

Let's always remember to tell of the resurrection whenever we have the opportunity to mention our faith, for it is the foundation upon which *all* our joy and hope is based in every corner of the planet.

Medical Pathology, Witch-Doctor Style

From Focus, Magazine of the Christian Medical-Dental Society of Canada.

DOCTORS going on short-term work trips abroad, and particularly to Africa or Haiti, may at first find their patient's complaints bear no resemblance to anything they learned in medical school. When I first went to West Africa sixty years ago, my confusion was compounded by having an interpreter who said he spoke English, but actually only spoke West African "pidgin" (Krio). I was told I wouldn't need an interpreter for my first patient, as he spoke Krio. All went well until I wanted him to sit up from a supine position on the couch. I could not make him budge with my entreaties to "sit up." In desperation I called for the interpreter, who addressed the patient in an apparent fury—Krio often sounds as if the speaker is in a fury—"E! Mbo! Yu no yeri wot in di doctor im se? I se yu fo siddon!" The patient meekly did that and sat up. (Krio is written phonetically.)

It was several months before I realized that, "When Ai de sit unda di pam tri ai no de si nuttin!," was a gynecological complaint, not an ophthalmologic one.

Dr. Hugh Maclure

Assuming that nowadays the interpreter is not a problem, some notes on animist views on the pathology of disease may help the doctor who is on a short visit to a less developed country. Examples are drawn mostly from Sierra Leone and Haiti.

1) Allah is behind all events; sometimes a long way behind, and there are many diseases which are simply due to His direct action, e.g., smallpox, leprosy and measles, among others.

2) Diseases may be due to the action of intermediaries, devils, witches, or secret enemies. Treatment of these require the attention of the witch-doctor, medicine man, shaman, houngoun or whatever his local name is. After paying the appropriate fee, he is then thought to be capable of neutralizing the evil (or good) spirit who is responsible. Certain witch-doctors are specialists in certain areas and against a particular devil that is thought to be causing the trouble. In this, they follow the same pattern as ourselves; Doctors may be general practitioners or specialists.

3) The spirits can be placated by gifts of money, food and sacrifices, such as chickens or goats and sometimes human beings. We saw several children who had been mutilated in sacrificial ceremonies. Other attempts at appeasement would be the wearing of protective charms or amulets, avoiding "holy" areas, keeping taboos and, of course, remunerating the witch-doctor for his advice. Animists would wear charms round their necks, wrists or ankles, often a goat's horn, leopard's claw or tooth, or something forged by the blacksmith. Muslims would wear little leather purses containing verses from the Koran. Many people in Sierra Leone wore both Muslim and animist charms, on the principle that insuring with Imperial Life *and* Manufacturers Life gives you better protection. I have had a "big" Muslim, who had made the trip to Mecca twice

and was therefore an *Alhadji*, ask me to write out a verse from the New Testament for him to add to the Koranic verse he already had in his amulet. There's nothing like playing it safe. The practical point of all this for the doctor from overseas is that if you see a patient festooned with these charms, it is very probable he or she has already been to the witch-doctor and is already taking the treatment prescribed by him and it may be the cause of his or her symptoms.

The witch-doctor could also be used to curse an enemy, and these curses—particularly the Islamic ones—were much feared in Sierra Leone. They were thought to cause various kinds of blindness, sterility, and abdominal diseases in the areas where we worked. In another chapter I have already mentioned the "holy donkeys" which were thought to ward off evil spirits.

In some cases, meningitis was thought to be due to being beaten on the head by a witch, leg ulcers to being bitten by a snake-spirit and various forms of tertiary yaws to similar events. (Yaws was virtually wiped out in the tropics twenty-five years ago, but may be returning.)

Local customs, too, can cause much illness, though this may not be readily admitted. Thus, kwashiorkor is often not due to food shortage so much as to harmful eating customs, e.g., fearing to give children eggs or fish; and vesico-vaginal fistula to delay in a late stage of labour because of outlet scarring from female circumcision. We saw almost nothing but harm and death from the use of "native medicine," in spite of the high regard anthropologists seem to have for these cultural treatments.

Other custom-caused conditions would be the burns sustained by epileptics who would not be fished out of the fire until they stopped convulsing, fractures unreduced and producing permanently deformed limbs or gangrene and death, and blindness from the application of various caustic substances.

The above notes won't help the short-termer much in any immediate way, so here are a few practical points to help him or her get over that first feeling of stunned homesickness when first confronted by fifty patients speaking six languages, none of which is understood by the wonder-working expert from over the sea. (I am assuming an assistant has triaged away the other hundred and fifty cases.)

- Love and patience are understood in any language and culture.

- Interpreters help best when simple direct questions are asked.

- *Always* make certain assumptions, with children particularly. Take it for granted that "native medicine" has been given, and that malaria, hookworm and probably a certain degree of malnutrition are present, too. In the British Colonial Medical Service where I worked during the war years, the monthly report forms only permitted one disease per patient—a perfect way of improving the official health of a country!

- Rely on signs more than symptoms and be patient. If the history doesn't make sense, functional inquiry is usually more helpful.

- Don't be put off by a mother's agitation when she sees you examining the right ear as well as the left, which is the one that is running.

- Joking and laughter helps ++++++.

- *Always touch* a child, even if you are baffled.

- You will probably have more opportunities to talk about your faith than at home. Take them.

- Pray aloud before any "procedure," large or small. Having an assistant speaking the language of the patient is a great help, of course, but if necessary do it yourself. I had a nurse in Africa

who always kept me humble. His prayer would go like this—
"O Lord, help in this operation and bring healing by Your
power, because the doctor is only human and it is up to You to
make sure the result will not be disastrous."

• If the opportunity to go on a work trip overseas comes up, take
it! You will never be the same again.

Dawn and Dusk, a Devotional

Thoughts on Numbers 10:35,36.

Whenever the Ark set out Moses said, "Rise up O Lord. May your enemies be scattered. May your foes flee before You." Whenever it came to rest, he said, "Return O Lord to the countless thousands of Israel" (NIV)

WHAT a way to start and finish the day! Because these words were addressed to the God of Israel, we won't be out of line in claiming them for ourselves since we, too, are Israelites, born again into the new Israel, the children of Abraham by faith. (Galatians 3; 28,29 6;12.)

Like Moses in the wilderness, I need to fix my thoughts and hopes on the Lord of Hosts first thing in the morning before the anxieties and distractions of the day submerge me like an incoming tide. This is often hard to do, since early morning is the time of day I feel particularly worm-like, and God seems particularly awesome and unattainable in His high and holy place.

Actually, I am facing a pseudo-problem, since my subjective feelings are not a true reflection of the situation. In reality, my feelings of inadequacy, far from keeping me apart from the Lord, ideally qualify me to come before Him as a supplicant.

This is where these verses have proved such a help to me at the beginning of the day. Said as a sort of reconnecting link between a half-asleep Christian and his wide-awake Lord, they conjure up a picture of Him walking ahead of me, shielding me from His, and my, enemies all through the day.

I was reminded vividly of this recently when I made a bicycle trip to Elk Island Park from Edmonton. That day it seemed that every buffalo in Alberta had parked itself on the road to the picnic area, and when I reached the gate of the park, I was glad that we had arranged to meet a van there. As we drove through the herds, the great beasts grudgingly scattered while I tucked in very close behind the vehicle, as invisible as possible.

In the same way, I can tuck in behind my Lord as He scatters the enemies of my soul all through the day: anxiety and fear, feelings of inadequacy, and guilt, false and real, and the great enemies of the Church worldwide.

At night I sometimes feel the Lord, still full of energy, has got too far ahead of me. Once again I am reminded of an event in my life. This time I am climbing in the mountains of North Wales as a small boy, with my father. As we scramble up Snowden, he gets ahead of me, and I call out, "Wait for me!" Even so the Lord hears my call in the evening and the connection is still there as He watches over the countless thousands of Israel (Revelation 7:9). This, too, becomes a good starting point for my evening time of prayer.

Regularly using these verses, morning and evening, has become a sort of formula which helps me to get started and to overcome the feeling that the God of the Universe might be unwilling to turn His attention to "such a worm as I." To have this sort of fixed point at which to start also overcomes the mood swings that we experience and which are so dependent on our state of health, blood sugar level, atmospheric pattern, time of the year and a host of other factors which have nothing whatever to do with our spiritual state, but which Satan tries to use.

Of course, my Anglican background makes me familiar with using a "set piece" as an aid to prayer or worship occasionally. The danger seems to be my tendency to use "set pieces" as a substitute, instead of an aid, in my prayers.

Verses such as this can also be used when interceding for others. A friend's name can be inserted—

O Lord, arise and let John's enemies be scattered. May he feel Your presence this evening as You watch over him and the countless other thousands of Israel.

Thank You, Lord!

Inspired by a Dinosaur— My Debt to C.S. Lewis

I realized C.S. Lewis was to be my model as a writer quite suddenly one night in 1946 on board a B17 Flying Fortress somewhere over the Atlantic Ocean. The plane had been adapted for passenger use, and was loaded with missionaries instead of bombs. The slow and noisy journey involved nights in Trinidad and Natal, Brazil. One got the impression the old lady needed rest stops as well as refuelling before we reached West Africa.

The flight was enlivened by our three sons, but they settled down and eventually slept peacefully in the converted bomb-bay. (I remember praying that they, too, would become instruments of peace, not destruction, when they grew up.)

During this journey, in fits and starts, I read *Miracles* by C.S. Lewis and there and then vowed I would never write another cliché, never again use two words when one would suffice, and *always* write from a Christian world view. To become a second "apostle to the agnostics," all I needed was imagination, inspiration, knowledge, experience, wit and ability. Ah, well, one had to start somewhere!

The life and writings of Dr. Clive Staples Lewis have probably generated a greater tonnage of paper in the form of theses, reviews, biographies, appreciation and criticism than any other Christian apologist this century. I therefore hesitate to add my puny nickel's worth to the collection. Yet, Professor Lewis has been my guide to a Christian world view and my example as a writer of English prose for over sixty-five years. If this makes me one of a crowd, so be it.

C.S. Lewis described himself as a relic from the Romantic Era, a living dinosaur in the modern world. In an inaugural lecture at Cambridge University in 1954, when appointed to the Chair of Medieval and Renaissance Literature, he presented himself as a rare specimen to be examined, rather than as a lecturer to be appreciated.[1] In fact, he was immensely appreciated in both capacities.

And what a specimen he was! A dragon's nest of politically incorrect ideas such as unabashed belief in the supernatural,[2] insistence on the reality of objective truth and the divine nature of reason and the moral law.[3] Worst of all, he was a believing Christian in the traditional sense. He added insult to injury by arguing powerfully against the opposites of his convictions. As he wrote, "Certain things, if not seen as lovely or detestable, are not being seen correctly at all."[4] Throughout his writings, lethal attacks are made against his old enemies—naturalism,[5] subjectivism,[6] and the irrationality of contemporary philosophies concerning human thought.[7] To the young Christian like myself, this Oxford professor appeared on the scene like an oasis in the desert. I accepted his views, so cogently expressed, as readily as a seal accepts the sea (he was, at first, a professor at Oxford).

Having found my writer's model three generations ago, a paradox has remained through the years; how could I have identified with a man so different from myself? Lewis was a bookworm if ever there was one—the "best read man in Europe," as has been said. Converted later in life from agnosticism, he described the event as "the steady unrelenting approach of Him whom I so earnestly desired *not* to meet."[8] He "loved monotony"[9] and spent nearly all his adult life in scholarship, reading, writing and teaching. For exercise, he walked and enjoyed swimming when opportunity arose (which was not often in England sixty years ago). He was a bachelor most of his life, and, in my view, made some of his worst generalizations on the subject of "falling in love" before he had actually experienced the calamity himself. He wrote, in his ignorance, "Who could bear to live in that excitement for even five years?"[10] He mistrusted machinery, hated organized games, and strongly contended that reason leads away from atheism to Christianity, rather than the reverse.[11] He wrote some of his most ferocious prose criticizing the school he attended (Malvern),[12] a criticism thoroughly unjustified according to his brother, Warren. He thrived in a sheltered world of books and scholarship. He was stirred to the depths by the music of Wagner and by Norse mythology.[13] He loathed hymns and was suspicious of extemporary prayer.[14]

Nearly all these characteristics describe a man with whom I have almost nothing in common. My education was semi-scientific and sadly lacking in the classics. I was happily converted at the age of twelve. I love games, the more organized the better. (Who wants a game with an incompetent referee?) I prefer people to books, hate monotony (which I have rarely experienced), and have had a honeymoon lasting sixty-two years. I greatly enjoy many hymns, can't abide Wagner's music and find most of Dickens and Shakespeare quite uninteresting (to my shame). I know little of Latin and nothing of Greek, and look back on my school days as very happy and productive. As a rabid health freak, I regard smoking as one of the great curses of our time and don't like the taste or the effect of alcohol (Lewis used both with enthusiasm). How ever could this man inspire both my life and my writing?

The answer to the puzzle lies not in the circumstances of Lewis' life, but in his world view and the constancy with which he expressed it. For a Christian growing up in the maelstrom of the twentieth century, this combination of remorseless integrity and imaginative prose was irresistible.

C.S. Lewis and his many biographers have given us an intimate account of his childhood in Belfast, his less than happy home life and his choice of a career and gradual establishment in the University of Oxford. In *Surprised By Joy*, all this is described in detail, and to me, his skill as a writer is once and for all established by the way he turns a life of skull-numbing dullness into a vivid and exciting story.

Surprised By Joy climaxes with his conversion—a reluctant surrender in which he was carried "kicking, struggling and resentful" into the enemies' camp after a long intellectual battle.[15] This was a profound change from deep atheism to deep Christianity. As a result, he was able to write about the doubts of the agnostic with insight and honesty.

With this background, C.S. Lewis set about addressing the cynical intellectual world of post-war England as few others have ever done. Never shifting from his Christian viewpoint, he wrote clearly, wittily and with immense scholarship, presenting "mere Christianity" to his own generation and generations to come. His writing covered a wide area: fantasy *(The Great Divorce, The Screwtape Letters, The Pilgrim's Regress)*, ancient myths retold *(Till We Have Faces)*, space fiction *(Perelandra, Out of the Silent Planet* and *That Hideous Strength)*, many learned treatises (e.g., *The Allegory Of Love, Paradise Lost)*, autobiography *(Surprised By Joy)*, and many other books, papers and essays on Christian, educational and philosophical subjects. His *Narnia* series of children's books are still bestsellers. He also wrote poetry, though it never gained the acclaim of his prose (and left me cold, compared to nearly all his other books).

Of Course I'm Biased

His first and best-known book was *The Screwtape Letters,* and this sets the pace for what followed. Knowing from the inside the agnostic's doubts and beliefs, Lewis was remorseless in taking presuppositions, whether Christian or atheist, to their logical conclusions. Much of his writing is devoted to this area of apologetics and the related subjects of the miraculous and objective truth. Not for him the "double-speak" of "lateral" thinking.

Three more elements in Lewis' writings must be mentioned. First, there is the constant sense of inconsolable longing.[16] This scent of Eden almost—but not quite—remembered, is one of the few things we had in common apart from Christianity. He described it as "Joy... which came riding back to me on huge waves of Wagnerian music and Norse or Celtic mythology."[17]. It was a feeling evoked by the beauty of nature, also, as, for instance, in his beloved County Antrim. For me, it rode on the waves of Bach, sometimes, and the mountains of North Wales and once, briefly, during the Caribou Marathon ski race! (Cynics, of course, have other explanations for this.) It is hard for a cold Scot to describe something so ephemeral; yet it was a Scot, George MacDonald, who first set C.S.L.'s longing on the right path, the search for holiness.[18]

Secondly, this hint of "longing" was not limited to his autobiography. It flavoured his imaginative writing also,[19] and what imagination! Who could forget the vivid pictures in his space trilogy? I have read these books at least five times each just for the descriptions of the final banquet or the guillotined head kept "alive" in *That Hideous Strength,* or the floating islands in *Perelandra.* Then there is Nature, described affectionately but vividly in *Miracles,* chapter nine, as a fellow creature. ("How could we ever have regarded her as 'Mother'"?) The *Narnia* books, too, invoke the feeling of longing, particularly with the "Aslan" passages. (Comparing Aslan, the true "Lion King," with Disney's

New Age substitute illustrates well the contrast between two world views.)

Thirdly, Lewis was a master of metaphor, the telling illustration or aphorism that wakes you up at the end of a long and closely reasoned passage. Surely he must be the most-quoted Christian writer of all time! He asks those who fail to recognize metaphor whether being as "harmless as doves" means "God expects Christians to lay eggs?" He points out that abandoning the idea of God as a Father arouses a mental picture of Him as a sort of cosmic gas or tapioca pudding, and "what if we don't like tapioca pudding?"[21] He states that in teaching ethics without the natural moral law, we "castrate and bid the geldings be fertile." [22] At what point does one stop quoting C.S. Lewis?

I believe the logic and world view of C.S. Lewis, and the ability to express it, are more than ever needed in the postmodern world; yet, those who know his writings are becoming an endangered species. For one who wants to correct this, I would suggest *The Screwtape Letters* as a start, for it will right away give a taste of the Lewis magic. If this appeals, I'd go straight to his most novel-like books, the space trilogy, for if they don't satisfy, I don't think the rest of C.S.L. will, either. However, if by now the addiction has begun, a feast lies in store.

Any writer who unashamedly proclaims the exclusive and fundamental *truth* of any philosophy or religion nowadays will, of course, be immediately criticized as intolerant, bigoted and hateful, particularly if it is Christianity that is being proclaimed. It comes as no surprise, therefore, that Lewis has been attacked and criticized by humanistic psychologists, literary critics and anyone alarmed at the wide influence his writings have had. The virulence of these attacks testifies, perhaps, to the soundness and good sense of his writing, though he does not easily fit into the mold of a "fundamentalist," even when the term is used in its original sense, as one believing in the fundamentals of Christianity. But his theology is another story. I am reminded that Christ said, *"He that is not against me is with me"* (Luke 9:50 my paraphrase).

I thank God for the many good and great people who have been my mentors. Not the least has been C.S. Lewis.

Endnotes: unless otherwise stated, the majority of sources are by C.S. Lewis.

[1]   *They Asked For A Paper,* Geoffrey Bles, 1962, pp. 24, 25.

[2]   *Miracles,* Collier Books, 1947 (The whole book).

[3]   *The Abolition Of Man,* The Macmillan Company, 1947 chapter 2.

[4]   Preface to *Paradise Lost,* Oxford University Press 1961, p. 53.

[5]   *Miracles,* ch. 2.

[6]   *Christian Reflections,* Eerdmans, 1967, p. 72.

[7]   *Ibid,* p. 61.

[8]   *Surprised By Joy.* Geoffrey Bles, 1955, p. 215.

[9]   Clyde S. Kilby, *A Mind Awake,* Geoffrey Bles, 1968, p. 10.

[10]   *Mere Christianity,* Collins Fontana Press, 1952, ch. 6.

[11]   Carolyn Keefe, *C.S. Lewis, Speaker and Teacher,* Zondervan, 1979, pp. 21, 22.

[12]   *Surprised By Joy,* ch. 6.

[13]   *They Asked For A Paper,* Geoffrey Bles, 1962, p.156.

[14]   *Letters,* Geoffrey Bles, 1966, p. 239, April '52.

[15]   *Surprised By Joy,* p. 215.

[16]   *Till We Have Faces,* Geoffrey Bles, 1956, p. 82.

[17]   *Surprised By Joy,* p. 157.

[18]   *Ibid,* p. 169.

[19]   *Till We Have Faces,* Introduction.

[20]   *Mere Christianity,* ch. 10.

[21]   *Miracles,* p. 74.

[22]   *The Abolition Of Man,* p. 16.

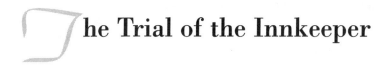

The Trial of the Innkeeper

A Christmas nightmare with a moral.

Characters in order of their apparition.

Judge.
Clerk of the Court.
Ben Judah, a Bethlehem Innkeeper.
Counsel for the Prosecution (P.C.).
David, a stableboy.
Counsel for the Defense (D.C.).
Us, perhaps.

Scene—a courtroom.

The Judge enters.

Clerk: All stand.

Judge: You may be seated.

Clerk: Mr. Ben Judah, you are charged with gross inhospitality to God Incarnate in that, during the year when all the world went to be taxed, you refused accommodation at your hotel to the King of Kings. How do you plead?

Ben Judah: Not guilty, my Lord.

Judge: You may proceed, Mr. Prosecutor.

Prosecuting Counsel: I call David, stableboy at The Slumberlodge, Bethlehem.

David takes the stand.

P.C.: Now, David, are you acquainted with Mr. Ben Judah?

David: Acquainted! I've worked my fingers to the bone for him, the miserable old slave-driver!

Defense Counsel: Objection!

Judge: Sustained. (*To clerk*) You will strike that remark from the records. (*To David*) You will confine yourself to answering the question in future.

P.C.: Tell us what happened the night the man, Joseph, and his wife, Mary, came to the inn.

David: Ben Judah says to me, "There's no room for any more. Tell 'em to try old Abe's place on the corner."

P.C.: He refused to let them stay at the inn, then?

David: You can say that again. Real mean old turkey 'e is, and…

D.C.: Objection!

Judge: Sustained. (*To David*) I'm not going to warn you again, young man.

P.C.: Then what happened?

David: Well the dame on the donkey, she says, "Oh please! I'm so tired. Isn't there anywhere we could stay here?"

P.C.: And did your master let them have a place in the inn then?

David: Are you kidding? "Take 'em around to the barn," he says. "I've had enough for one night." Then he slams the door in their faces!

P.C.: Thank you. Your witness, Counsellor.

Defense Counsel: David, on the night in question, is it true you were under notice of dismissal for stealing?

P.C.: Objection! That question is incompetent, irrelevant and completely immaterial.

D.C.: (*To the judge*) On the contrary, Your Honour; I intend to establish bias in this witness.

Judge: Objection overruled. You may continue, Counsellor.

D.C.: Answer the question, David.

David: Well—er—I suppose I did *borrow* a few things occasionally.

D.C.: I put it to you that, in fact, you stole from your master anything that was not actually nailed down!

P.C.: Objection. Counsel is leading the witness.

D.C.: I withdraw the question. Is it true, David, that your master had actually forgiven you five times?

David: I suppose so.

D.C.: Now about this evening we've been discussing. Was Bethlehem crowded?

David: You can say that again! Talk about 'silent night.' Everyone had come to be taxed, see? I think them taxes are wick—

D.C.: Never mind what you think. Was the inn then actually full up?

David: Of course, but...

D.C.: Was it usual for your master to turn away travellers?

David: 'E'd 'ave put up Old Nick himself so long as 'e paid in advance!

Judge: Silence in court. That will do, young man!

D.C.: Was it usual for him to make up a bed in the stable for travellers?

David: No.

D.C.: In other words, he went to great pains to accommodate his guests, wouldn't you say?

David: (*No answer*)

D.C.: I have no further questions for this witness at this time.

P.C.: I have no other witnesses, but I would remind you that the general public has, for centuries, agreed that the innkeeper was greatly to be condemned, and by his lack of hospitality missed a wonderful opportunity to go down in history as the man who entertained the King on His birthday.

D.C.: I intend to show that he did no such thing, and at this time I would like to put Mr. Ben Judah himself on the stand.

(B.J. is sworn in)

D.C.: I believe your inn is nearly always full, is that correct?

B.J.: Yes sir, we have a number of regular guests.

D.C.: Were you full on the night in question?

B.J.: Full right up. It was tax time, you know.

D.C.: Could you have found a room for this couple in the house if you had known the circumstances?

B.J.: Not without turning one of the other guests out of his room, and I didn't like to do that. In fact, I don't think the King of Kings would have wanted me to do it, either.

D.C.: Now, this stable they spent the night in. Was it comfortable?

B.J.: Well, it was warm and fairly clean, and sheep and cows are better company than some humans, you know.

D.C.: I have no further questions.

P.C.: But I have a few. Now, sir, do you deny that you failed to give the King of Kings a place to sleep in your hotel?

B.J.: I gave Him the best I had at the time, and later, when I knew who He was, I gave Him the whole of myself, my sin and my life. I was among the five hundred who saw Him alive after He rose from the dead. Have *you* given yourself to Him, Mr. Prosecutor?

P.C.: I object to that question! *I* am not on trial here!

Judge: On the contrary—the birth of this baby has put us all on trial. This is a pertinent question, and I would like to see it pursued.

B.J.: I have been accused for centuries of refusing to take the King of Kings into my house. Is He in *your* house, Mr. Prosecutor?

P.C.: (*Pulling a prepared statement out of his pocket and reading it rapidly*) I have a high regard for the spirit of Christmas. I send my children to Sunday School sometimes. My Christmas decorations are the finest on the block. I never cheated anyone who had not cheated me first. I even go to church myself when my other commitments allow me to do so. I'm not a hypocrite like so many—

Judge: What commitments, Counsellor?

P.C.: I have curling in the winter and my golf in the summer, and I often am up late on Saturday night, and I have to get my sleep on account of my health. Then again, weekends are the only time I have for recreation with my family, Your Honour. One can go overboard on this religious business, you know. Christmas is all very well, of course. It's the children's festival, I always say, and the Christmas spirit certainly does improve business, but....

Judge: The Christmas baby was tortured to death by adults, Counsellor.

P.C.: Respectfully, Your Honour, I don't think we should get morbid. This is the Season of Good Cheer. Think of the manger, holly, shepherds, angels, Santa, staff parties, reindeer, cash registers ringing. I mean, Christmas bells ringing—it's beautiful, beautiful. Why, oh why, didn't He stay a baby? I try to ignore the rest of it, but sometimes when things aren't going too well.... Ahem, excuse me, Your Honour. But as I was saying, who is on trial here anyway?

Judge: That's fairly obvious, Counsellor. Case dismissed.

Mid-Winter Night's Dream

THE room was warm, the Christmas dinner had been well up to its usual standard, and as I sat in my armchair, planning to fill out a passport application form, I found myself idly looking at a Christmas card with a picture of the manger scene on it. As I struggled to bring it into focus, the shadows and colours began to grow more vivid; the Holy Light around the Mother and Child shone brighter, and I heard for the first time the lusty cry of a newborn baby. (That line in the carol, *"But little Lord Jesus, no crying He makes"* always struck me as unreal!) There was a rich farmyard smell, and the straw which had looked so clean and comfortable on the Christmas card turned into real straw—cold, damp in places and a bit prickly. Mary looked exhausted and yet radiant.

The animals, who had been looking gravely at the Infant and His mother, wandered away to a corner, and I followed them. They began to converse in low voices, chewing and flicking their tails. Joseph's donkey was the first to speak. It appeared that he was well respected, and was a direct descendant of Balaam's ass. They ignored me as I drew nearer to listen.

Donkey: I told you God was coming into the stable. Wise men are on their way to worship Him.

First sheep: Yes, they say He is the Lamb of God who will take away the sin of the world.

Second sheep: Now our own lambs will be saved from the altar.

First goat: Saved, my hoof! Who ever saw a god with flies buzzing round him on a bed of straw?

Cow: What's wrong with straw, and why shouldn't flies buzz?

Second goat: (*striking a dignified posture*) If that is what your God is like I'll have nothing to do with Him, thank you.

Donkey: You have no choice. You have to take Him as He is, not as you imagine Him to be.

Horse: (*shaking his head*) I'm not very bright, I know, but surely there is something different about this baby. I believe He really is God and will redeem us all.

Second goat: Which god? At the latest count, there were ninety-six official deities and thousands of unofficial ones.

(*I could not help feeling I'd heard those goats before. Could it have been on a CBC TV program somewhere?*)

Donkey: We always invent gods until we meet the Living God Himself. But who cares what we think? That Baby is what God thinks.

Cow: If He goes about claiming to be God, they'll soon kill Him and that will be that.

First goat: (*looking very wise*) Isn't all this talk about God rather embarrassing in this day and age? Surely scientific advances and modern thought have made all that sort of thing irrelevant now. Not that I'm against the *idea* of God.

Donkey: Why not?

First goat: What do you mean, "Why not?"

Donkey: If there is no God, the *idea* of God can only foster delusion and ignorance, surely?

First goat: I don't know, it might make people act more kindly.

Second goat: Nonsense—there is no God. The universe is irrational and evolved by chance. Everything is basically absurd.

Donkey: Everything?

Second goat: Of course. Be logical.

Donkey: Then your statement is absurd, too.

Second goat: Now look here! Are you calling me stupid?

Donkey: No, merely absurd. Isn't that what you just said?

Horse: (*shaking his head*) There must be something different about this Baby. They never argue like this over others.

Donkey: I, for one, am prepared to believe this Baby is God Himself, come to earth for some special purpose which I admit I do not understand.

First goat: These idiots make me sick. Let's hope humans will have more sense.

Cow: Don't worry, they'll murder Him and no one will remember Him in fifty years, more's the pity.

Donkey: (*placidly munching hay*) They may kill Him, alright, but that won't be the end of Him. God will work something out, you'll see.

First goat: (*in disgust*) Holy cow!

Cow: Yes?

First goat: Not you, Stupid!

Sheep: How will He save His people from their sins? We poor sheep get slaughtered every day without that getting accomplished.

Second goat: Those humans aren't going to like that bit of dogma one little bit. Saved because they're so good and clever, okay, but saved because they are so bad and sinful? That will go over like a lead balloon!

First goat: Yes, of course. However, we must hope the Christmas myth survives, because it would be good for business, and the pretty manger scenes delight the children.

Second goat: Right! A beautiful story, and throw in the crazy reindeer with the red nose from time to time if it starts to rub a bit thin. At all costs, let's hope people will stop thinking about a real God who *does* things. Can you think of anything more undignified? Actually taking on human form and entering the world yelling, blue in the face and blood-smeared like any other mammal! How awful if it were really true!

First goat: Don't talk like that—it makes me nervous. Think of God as a vague spiritual influence, like a sort of gas. Gases don't make demands on us. That Baby might.

Second goat: Well, He'll probably be dead in thirty years or so, and we'll be left in peace.

The two goats wandered away, but I saw them eyeing the Baby nervously from time to time. The other animals approached the Holy Family. Joseph patted the donkey's neck and one of the sheep leaned forward and hesitantly licked the Baby's little button nose. Mary was looking better now and her face was filled with awe. Joseph pulled something from the folds of his cloak. "If you are strong enough now, dear," he said, "Perhaps you could help me fill out this tax form of Caesar's. Why they make these things so incomprehensible, I'll never know."

The application form in my hand gradually came into focus again and the barn dissolved into the picture on the Christmas card once more. The unreality of the dream was replaced by the reality of the modern world. It was a place of turmoil, and confusion, a far cry from the rural peace of the manger. Yet the conflicts and savagery we were reading about daily increasingly fulfilled the prophecies about the Christmas Baby who was coming again. Meanwhile, I had forms to fill in, work to do and a life to live. I was glad, though, to have entered the stable for a brief glimpse of that wonderful day. I plan to visit there again next year, God willing.

A Prolonged Grief

Enlarged from an article in
"Physician" magazine, Sept. 1998.

IN 1992, our youngest son died of AIDS, aged forty-five.

Andrew was born in a West African village, delivered by his father. His first eight years were spent as a "missionary kid," with all the stresses, good and bad, that such a life involves. He was bright, healthy, athletic and popular. From grade nine on, he attended a Christian school, then did a year at the University of Alberta before entering Bible school for three years. During this time he studied, played hockey, sang in a quartet and toured with the chorale. He was student body president in his last year there. We had no idea of the storm clouds gathering in the mind of our "golden boy" at this time. In fact, our ignorance of what was troubling him then was one of the added griefs when the storm broke.

After this Andrew got into medical school at U of A. We noticed that study, so easy for him in the past, was getting pretty hard. During this time, we went to Uganda for a year and he came with us for a couple of months, getting a preview of surgery and other medical procedures.

Dr. Hugh Maclure

In Andrew's final year as a medical student, his turmoil increased and at times, we found out later, he had felt suicidal. We knew nothing of this, though when we returned, we noticed he only came to church when we invited him and he seemed to have fewer and fewer Christian friends. His lack of spiritual growth at this time was the "beginning of sorrows" for us.

The second blow fell when he was an intern. He had been in the family practice program and we had talked about him perhaps joining us in our practice. However, at this time he switched to anesthesia and then told us he was a homosexual. That weekend was the bleakest we can remember. We spent it on one of the Gulf Islands, and fasted, prayed and wept. (Being an unemotional Scotsman, it was the first time I had wept for years!) We each lost five or six pounds in weight in a few days.

From that time on, we felt as if we were in a swamp of disappointment, and though we still stood on the Rock, it seemed a long, long way down. Andrew's lifestyle was like a sliver under the nail that one cannot remove or ignore. We no longer shared the most important things in life, and in spite of our efforts to be accepting and loving parents, Andrew increasingly felt more and more ill-at-ease in our company. We continued to hold on to the Lord's covenant promises and we prayed for our son, morning, night and through the day.

We know Andrew struggled for some time to reconcile the conflicting claims of a "gay" lifestyle with the biblical view of life, and even, for a short time, attended a "gay" church, though, to his credit, not for long. Eventually he made his choice, turning his back on Christianity. How much, if any, of the Christian teaching he knew so well he retained, we do not know; but he told us later that, after "coming out of the closet," he plunged deeply into the promiscuous, drug-using homosexual subculture. His failing the final exams in his specialty several times before actually passing was due, he felt, to taking marijuana before the tests to calm his nerves.

The third blow came in 1986, when Andy wrote to us saying that his partner had AIDS and that he, himself, was HIV-positive. Could this really be happening to our lovely son? God was allowing us to get a glimpse of the torment He went through when the world rejected His only Son and the sins of the world were laid on His shoulders.

Andrew began to fill his life with adventures, knowing that his life on earth would be short. He went through the Grand Canyon on a raft, ran in the Portland Marathon and kept himself in good shape by cycling, climbing, hiking and swimming. (He had been a member of the U. of A. swimming team.) All this probably delayed the remorseless course of his disease.

Andrew's partner died in 1987 and his grief was overwhelming. About this time he wrote us an angry letter, expressing his hurt that we would not give up our traditional prejudices against homosexuality and held on to our biblical view of sexual morality so strongly. We wrote back reaffirming our love and acceptance of him as our greatly loved son and pointing out that stubbornness was a two-way street. If he could find no middle ground where he could accept both historical Christianity and the postmodern view of life, we, too, had the same dilemma. After this we had no more communication with him for about eight months until finally he got in touch with us again. Later he told us he had come to see our point of view, particularly as his disease progressed.

A year after his bereavement, Andrew began to write us regular reports on his condition and the slow deterioration monitored by his anaemia, falling "helper T-cell" count and decreasing exercise tolerance. Skin and other minor problems occurred as pre-AIDS syndrome developed and he was put on AZT, which about that time began to be used earlier than had at first been advised.

Blow number four now fell upon us. It was suggested to us that Andrew's condition had probably been caused or aggravated by shortcomings in our parenting. What parent doesn't already feel inadequate in the first place? The fact that Andrew himself emphatically denied attributing his homosexuality to his "MK" upbringing helped a bit, but not much. Again we could only hang on to the known and proven grace, love, mercy and sovereignty of the LORD, but we began to pray more intensely for the coming of the day when reconciliation and restoration of joy and peace would take place.

The answer began in part to take place as Andrew deteriorated. He gave up his work as an anesthetist while he was still competent and safe, and took a leave of absence, hoping for perhaps another two or three good years, but it was not to be.

Just before quitting, he came for an unusually long visit, seeming to be more at ease with himself and us than he'd been for many years. We walked together along a trail in the mountains overlooking Okanagan Lake and talked together about our love for him and sorrow at what was happening. He reaffirmed his love for us and said he had come, in part, to understand how we must feel about a lifestyle that had landed him in the situation he now faced. He stayed three days and we swam and cycled together, though it was sad to see how soon he tired and how easily I kept up in the water with this man who had been leaving me in his wash when swimming ever since the age of twelve. During the next twelve months, we were to see more of Andrew than in the previous eighteen years.

A few weeks later, Andrew went on a trip abroad where he picked up a 'flu-like illness from which he never really recovered. Then came, one after the other, like hyenas sensing a meal, the opportunistic infections of full-blown AIDS. He struggled through the summer of 1991, taking frequent blood transfusions and other treatments involving $1,500 worth of drugs a month.

In July, with great difficulty, he came up to see us at Kelowna, on the way to visit a friend at Calgary. It was immediately obvious that he was very ill indeed and soon after he reached us, he began hallucinating and acting strangely. We sat up with him one night while he wept and raved for an hour, then settled down and more of his despair, feelings of love for us and grief at his partner's death came to the surface as well as his basic conviction that God was Love. Instead of driving on to Calgary next day, I flew back to Vancouver with him, and he was immediately admitted to St. Paul's hospital where a diagnosis of cortisone overdose was made and he began to improve quickly.

Once his medications were adjusted, Andrew put on twenty-five pounds and enjoyed a few months of "Indian Summer," regaining much of his old strength, though it was clear his judgement was much impaired. I remember him discussing with me whether or not he should trade in his twenty-year-old BMW and buy a new one!

We saw much of Andrew that fall of 1991 and wish now we had seen more. I think we had not realized how completely he had come back to us and no longer guarded his privacy as he had in the past. We got to know our way around his apartment in Vancouver as we stayed with him, cooking his favourite meals, watching his favourite TV programs and meeting his many homosexual friends.

Christmas 1991 was a really good time. Andrew came up from the coast and his elder brother and family came from Edmonton and joined us at Kelowna. Andy was even able to do a little cross-country skiing; but it was the very last tango. After his brother and family returned to Edmonton, he stayed on with us and seemed unwilling to return home. His grief at all he was losing was very evident. It was hard to say goodbye to him at Kelowna airport, and we arranged to come to Vancouver and see him soon and, in fact, whenever he gave us the call. About that time he began to tell his friends he was tired of the struggle and wanted to die.

The call came in mid-February, and by the time we got there he was already in the hospital, a place that held no terrors for him. At that time a CT brain-scan showed the signs of an AIDS-related tumour. We spent the last four weeks of his life with him during the day and I slept on the floor of his room during his last night. I was able, during those weeks, to act as a sort of intermediary between him and the nursing staff as he gradually lost the power to communicate. His last spontaneous sentences were "I'm so glad you're here," and "It's come so soon." Both his brothers came to see him, as well as two nephews and a niece, his eldest brother making the trip from Australia to do so.

During Andrew's year at university, he had one Christian friend, a fellow member of the Golden Bears swimming team and now an orthopoedic surgeon. This friend came to spend the day with Andrew twice during his last weeks, though the two friends had lost touch with each other for many years. Dr. Penny talked and prayed with Andrew, who accepted this with gladness.

The sixth blow came as a happy release on March 21, 1992.

When his partner died, Andrew made a will and directed that his own funeral should be a secular one, though we know at the end he wanted to change the arrangements but could not tell us in what way. We carried out his wishes but felt that the funeral, though secular, should also make mention of the stresses in Andy's Christian family and upbringing. We therefore asked one of Andrew's homosexual friends to be master of ceremonies and also gave an opportunity for as many of them to give a tribute as wanted to do so. When the time came, they were all quite unable to speak. I knew five or six of them were waiting for the same fate to overtake them and a funeral was a terrifying preview.

Andrew's brother told of Andrew's life, not omitting his exposure to Christianity, and Dr. Penny, the orthopoedic surgeon friend, gave a eulogy. We had asked him to bring out something of the Christian view of life and death, bearing in mind most of those attending would have agnostic or New Age beliefs. Near the end of his speech, he said, "I am grateful I have a faith in a risen Jesus and in the God of the Bible, which has given me a hope and a confidence, and just a little glimpse of that world beyond this life. I feel confident that Andrew's spirit is safe and secure and nurtured; that he is unconditionally accepted for exactly who he is and that he is experiencing a peace and joy and wholeness that he never experienced here on earth."

We must interject here that we believe our Andrew's soul is in good hands. He did at one time, as far as we can see, put his whole trust in Jesus Christ. (But in these matters we really can't see very far.) We do not know what was going through his mind in the last few weeks. We read to him from the Word of God and prayed with him each night at the hospital. He seemed to like this, though it was hard to tell how he was feeling as he gradually became semi-conscious. We know, too, that the LORD of all the earth will do what is right, and when we see Him face to face, we will rejoice over all His decisions in the place where there are no regrets.

About a dozen of our friends, most of whom did not even know Andrew, drove over three hundred miles to be with us on that day, and their love and presence were of immense comfort. Nearly one hundred cards and letters came from friends, including a number from Andrew's own circle. Some of these sought to comfort us by denying that Andrew had really gone, though the idea that he was part of a sunbeam or a dewdrop on the grass was thin comfort compared to the Christian hope of the resurrection. Here Dr. Penny's comments are worth quoting in full:

Dr. Hugh Maclure

I believe the Lord would have you know how much He cherishes you and your lives poured out for Him. He wants you to know that Andrew's spirit is His concern and His treasure. He loved Andrew enough to die for him, and He loves you enough to honour your prayers for him. He is ever our intercessor. I have been thinking much of the life of Jesus recently. The image of Him dying on the cross between the two criminals to me represents the extent of His mercy, so far exceeding this world's. He granted paradise, knowing the thief's heart, extending mercy and not judgement. When Lazarus died, He knew He was about to raise him from the dead, yet, on meeting the grief-stricken sisters He wept. He shared their sorrow, felt their pain and shared their emotions. 'Yea, though I walk through the valley…' He weeps with us today. Yes, He is the God of eternity, the God in control. Andrew's life is hid in Him. I trust the Lord explicitly with Andrew's eternity. His justice and mercy are so vast as to be unfathomed.

Let us trust in the seed of faith sown by yourselves and the Holy Spirit and trust also in the power of prayer, I have been praying much for Andrew these past few weeks, asking the Lord to honour your prayer and integrity—in His name's sake. Bless you, in Jesus' name. May you know Him more dearly at this time.

Blessed are those who have friends like ours.

We have written at length on the course of Andrew's dying. A prolonged grief, perhaps more than a sudden catastrophic one, gives one time to think about the various elements that make up grief. C.S. Lewis, writing in the storm of his sorrow when his wife died, noted the similarity between grief and fear, and we know what he meant—the dry mouth, loss of appetite, restlessness and racing thoughts (with periods of blank apathy).

Grief is agonizing. Even to write about Andrew at this distance blurs the eyes. We have mentioned how it needs human comfort. It also needs the resolution of guilt, whether real or imagined. "What did we do wrong?" is the cry uttered by millions of parents throughout the world's history. Being overseas missionaries involved sacrifices for us and also for our children. (But they had no choice!) Perhaps Andrew's ruined life was the result of our sacrificing him... but then again, perhaps not. What did Christ really mean when He said following Him would cause rifts in families? (Luke 14:26... Matthew 10:34–38.)

Intense introspection does not help, and we have come more and more to ignore our feelings, instead doggedly claiming the sovereignty of God. This is very far from being a heroic stance. It isn't stoicism of the classical variety, far less that of the Kubler-Ross type. Instead it is the opposite—a complete acknowledgement that we are at the end of our resources, then waiting for God in His boundless grace to heal our broken hearts and change our feelings at whatever time He sees fit. And He really does this! We begin to remember that there are others who love us and whom we love, that there are bills to pay, things to do and responsibilities to shoulder again. There may even be a chance to do better another time.

Since Andy died, we have been enabled to tell others with conviction that God's comfort and presence are real, His grace sufficient, His restoration complete and His way perfect. Our whole family has been drawn closer together. A day does not pass without Andrew being in our thoughts, but the pain is bearable now and the positive things are beginning to show themselves, like shoots of grass through the devastation left by the eruption of Mt. St. Helens—and volcanic soil is rich and fertile eventually.

Some study notes on Micah contained these words:

We may not understand why... He lets such terrible things happen to us, whether through 'natural disasters' or through self-inflicted calamities. But we know the Lord of great reversals is working His purposes out... and Paul reminds us that those purposes are to make us more like Christ, and to lead us to glory.

on't Confuse Me With the Facts

THIS article is written rather reluctantly, on request, to follow Chapter 28. I warn you, it will be technical, boring, controversial and a pain in the neck to write. It may also, in a year or two, be illegal. It is hard to find the balance between being honest and inoffensive at the same time.

The previous chapter tells of homosexuality and its repercussions in one family; but what of homosexuality in the social context? The loaded words "intolerance," "bigoted hatred" and "prejudice" fill the air as soon as the subject is mentioned, and a cloud of misinformation fogs the conversation (and the news media).

In this atmosphere, the search for understanding, information and impartial investigation is immediately labeled a hate-inspired activity, and the publicizing of scientific research (unless its findings are supportive of the homosexual's claims) is considered merely another example of homophobia. This meaningless word is taken to describe both fear and/or hatred of homosexuals and homosexuality, i.e., a threat to their human rights. Actually my attitude—and that of most of the Christians I know—towards a homosexual friend is far more threatening and obnoxious. I love the friend and am profoundly sorry for him or her. One cannot watch the misery of one's own son without having these feelings. But of course, homosexuals do not want sympathy or compassion. They want *complete* acceptance.

Any piece of writing which challenges homosexual propaganda is ipso facto labeled hate literature. The fact that it may be true is no excuse! At least two high-profile Alberta doctors found this out a few years ago when they each, in their own areas, called for the dangers of the homosexual lifestyle to be explained in schools whenever that lifestyle was promoted there as "safe and natural." Both were roasted by the media and reprimanded by their medical association. When they asked why the CMA, of all people, should object to the spreading of medical information (which the CMA itself knew to be true), they were told that the truth of the information was not in question. Mentioning it at all was the problem, because it fomented intolerance!

A perfect example of the lunacy that puts political correctness before the protection of our childrens' health and happiness.

Writing these notes is at present legal, but it may not be so in a few months, so I will hurry along and try to keep my remarks kind. However, the last time my words on this subject were printed, they aroused the wrath of homosexual psychiatrists both in Calgary and Edmonton. One of Andrew's friends, who did not attend his funeral, wrote a personal letter to me saying he was glad Andy was dead so he would no longer have to put up with the company of his bigoted and homophobic father! He was so far off the mark that I did not bother to reply.

Homosexuality—Introduction

In these notes, "HS" will denote "homosexual" or "homosexuality" for brevity. I do not like to use the word "gay." My son used to be gay in the real sense. Then he began to practice homosexuality.

The current humanistic or "liberal" view of HS arises from philosophical, not scientific, roots. It rests on at least three pre-suppositions:

1) Sexual behaviour has nothing to do with morality (a denial of "Natural Law" that states certain things are wrong or right *in themselves*).

2) Sexual behaviour is a matter of civil rights, not ethics. Thus, HS subjects are victims, not perverts.

3) Both the above propositions become part of a larger issue making "sexual freedom" a political rather than a behavioural issue. The extreme political left (Herbert Marcuse, William Klein) would carry this to the extreme of destroying family life so that atheistic socialism can take over the resulting anarchy. The above statements are justified by appeals to:

   (a) scientific studies,
   (b) social studies, and
   (c) philosophical arguments.

We should challenge them on all three grounds, but on the *first two first*. Few proponents of secular humanism are interested in Christian and biblical philosophical arguments. (I am not suggesting this should *always* be our tactic when witnessing.) With HS friends, let *them* choose the ground on which to argue, but if you do, it is important to know the facts of the case, even if they are confusing!

The case for HS rests on five assumptions:

1) HS is inborn (genetic); therefore, sexual "orientation," not "choice."

2) Ten percent of the population is HS.

3) HS is a healthy, normal lifestyle.

4) HS is no danger to children.

5) HS is an unchangeable condition.

HS is genetic

The evidence for this was originally reported by Kallman, in 1952, who found that when one identical twin was HS, the other was, too, in 100 percent of cases. His results have never been repeated in innumerable series since. For instance, a study reported in the *British Journal of Psychiatry* in 1992 found that in only twenty percent of cases was the second identical twin HS. Since identical twins have identical DNA, anything less than 100 percent correlation is fatal to the theory that, inevitably, "my genes made me HS."

Lavay (1992) claimed to find a minute anatomical difference in the mid-brain of some HS subjects, compared with "normal" subjects. In 1993 *"Science"* reported similar findings in a certain area of the DNA strand. Other familial associations and variations have been found or suggested, marking differences between HS subjects and the general population. For instance, left-handedness is very slightly commoner in HS subjects, and mothers who are infertile or who come from infertile families are slightly more likely to bear HS children. Slight differences in fingerprints have also been observed, according to some workers.

Biologists have observed HS behaviour, particularly but not exclusively, in female animals from fruit flies to Japanese Macac monkeys and bonobos, for instance. This uncommon finding has been taken by some as proof of a genetic basis for HS. Others point out the influence of factors such as stress, pleasuring and submissive behaviour. In fact, a full range of human activity—whether admirable, immoral, commendable or criminal—could be justified if we appeal to what happens in the animal kingdom.

There is immense pressure to prove a genetic basis for HS, which will forever establish the proposition that "he can't help it, he was born like that." The scanty evidence does suggest there may be a familial *tendency* towards HS as one of many factors, such as nurturing, environment, choice, etc., just as there is in alcoholism, which itself has a host of features resembling HS. More about this later.

Research trying to establish a connection between the genes and HS runs into many problems. First, it is research usually conducted with the desire or intention to support a party line. Second, there is the awkward fact that "correlation is not causation"—in other words, carrying a briefcase in Africa does not cause appendicitis (though that condition is commoner among those who do carry one), and being tall does not cause one to become a basketball player. Again, many researchers have pointed out that the anatomical changes found by some workers could have been *caused* by HS, rather than the other way around.

On top of this controversy lies the fact there has never been and never will be an experiment to measure the strength (or existence) of free will in choice. Furthermore, those who most strongly urge the genetic basis of HS appear equally strongly to deny the same courtesy to heterosexuals, who must also have a genetic basis for their "orientation," feelings and so-called "homophobia." And, of course, there are agnostics who are not slow to carry their deterministic theories about behaviour to their logical conclusions. Thus, William Provine wrote in 1988, "Free will as it is traditionally conceived—freedom to make uncoerced and unpredictable choices among alternative possible courses of action—simply does not exist." Such willingness to take one's presuppositions (almost) to their logical conclusion is very refreshing, but does not encourage discussion!

Dr. Hugh Maclure

HS subjects are ten percent of the general population

This was first proposed by Kinsey, the father of phoney scientific studies. He found in the general population that ten percent showed some HS activity over three years, eight percent showed exclusive HS activity over three years, and four percent showed exclusive HS activity all their lives. In other words, he claimed a figure of four percent for exclusively HS people in a lifetime, not ten percent; but the HS lobby, and hence the media, insist in quoting the ten percent figure. Incidentally, Kinsey used volunteers, many of whom were prison inmates, some of them sex offenders.

Even the four percent figure has been found to be excessive. Subsequent studies, including one at least that excluded Christians and Jews (!), have come up with figures ranging from one percent to four percent. A British study in 1989 found only 1.7 percent of males had ever had HS intercourse, and less than half of those had ever had it more than once. These statistics, denying as they do HS lobby claims, are hotly contested by HS activists. I suspect the real figure for exclusive HS subjects could be as high as 2.5 percent and rising as acceptance and encouragement of the condition increases. In ancient Rome, I'm told, nineteen out of the first twenty Caesars were HS or bisexual. This was in a society that tolerated and expected HS, among the wealthy at least.

HS is a healthy, normal lifestyle

Kinsey (again) found a group of HS subjects to be well-adjusted by comparison with heterosexuals. I think we could go further than that. A friend of mine now disabled with MS has more than once told me that when he was working for a government department, claiming to be HS was the road to promotion. Be that as it may, Kinsey's subjects were chosen by the HS lobby then still further selected by the investigator.

Of Course I'm Biased

In 1973, the American Psychiatric Association removed HS from its list of psychiatric disorders. This was a political decision under intense pressure from a noisy crowd of HS activists outside the building. Forty percent of psychiatrists present voted against the motion, and of 2,500 psychiatrists surveyed in 1977, nearly two-thirds said HS subjects had more trouble forming loving relationships and that their troubles were due to personal problems, not societal stigma.

Actually, the health dangers are so horrendous they embarrass even the HS activists. There are figures showing that HS men, at least, have a greatly increased risk of suicide, alcoholism, drug abuse, depression, sexually transmitted diseases including, of course, AIDS, hepatitis B, "gay bowel syndrome," etc., not to mention early death. HS is a MASSIVE threat to public health. Thomas Schmidt's book, *Straight and Narrow* (Inter-Varsity Press, 1995) has a chapter on the health complications of HS followed by fifteen pages containing well over 120 references supporting the evidence that HS is, to say the least, a very grave health risk, and these references are largely drawn from ethically and morally "neutral" journals such as the *British Medical Journal*, the *New England Journal of Medicine*, etc.

HS poses no threat to children

HS advocates often quote the fact that seventy percent of sexual assaults on young children involve heterosexuals. This means that thirty percent involve HS subjects. No further comment needed. In other words, the impression that the offences against children reported on the news seem to involve HS subjects quite often is a true one.

There are HS extremists out there, such as the members of NAMBLA (North American Man-Boy Love Association), but it might be unfair to take them too seriously. After all, Christian extremists shoot abortionists very occasionally. However, abortionist-shooters incur the condemnation of the vast majority of practicing Christians, and their activities are seen as bringing disgrace on Christ and His followers. I have not noticed the same condemnation of NAMBLA and its activities among HS spokesmen (though Andrew, my HS son, had nothing good to say about them).

Many HS lobbyists claim that sex for or with children is a basic human right, and that shielding children from sexual abuse is interfering with civil rights, not protecting society. Thus, Svend Robinson at the Vancouver HS games in 1990: "The diversity of HS community is good," and NAMBLA: "Children must break the yoke of parental protection." Intellectuals may promote the ideals of the lunatic fringe more or less genteelly, but Michael Swift in *Gay Community News,* Feb. 5, 1987, wrote perhaps more honestly:

"We shall sodomize your sons… we will seduce them in your schools, in your dormitories, in your gymnasiums, in your locker rooms, in your sports arenas, in your seminaries, in your youth groups, in your movie theatres and bathrooms… wherever men are together. All laws banning HS will be revoked. Be careful when you speak of HS because we are always among you. The family unit will be abolished. All churches who condemn us will be closed. Our only gods are handsome young men."

Of course, these are extremist statements with which most HS subjects would hotly disagree. I think, though, that they deserve the epithet "Normophobic" at least as often as the word "Homophobe" describes those who see moral and physical dangers in homosexuality.

HS is unchangeable

There is no evidence for this statement and plenty for its opposite. Since, however, a prerequisite to change is that both patient and therapist must be committed to change, it is small wonder that

HS psychiatrists can report they have never seen change! Actually the notion that HS is unchangeable is simply a repeat of assumption number one—"HS is genetically determined."

In his book, *Homosexuality and the Politics of Truth* (Baker Books, 1996), Dr Satinover, M.D., a psychiatrist, lists on page 186 nine studies with an average overall success rate of over fifty percent (success being defined as "considerable to complete change"). This was in HS subjects who wanted to change. Meanwhile, strident advocates continue to proclaim that HS is natural, normal, inborn, unchangeable, healthy, desirable and to be encouraged and protected. Richard Isay, M.D., has chaired an American Psychiatric Association Committee on the Abuse and Misuse of Psychiatry, and has opposed all attempts to change HS subjects by counselling, even when the subjects themselves request it. He says that change *never* takes place, and stories to the contrary are driven by homophobia in bigoted, dishonest and abusive therapists. He further calls for such therapists to be "quarantined" and denied employment. I know psychiatrists in both Edmonton and Calgary who agree with him, though in less abusive terms.

Miscellaneous notes

Most authorities seem to agree that HS arises in families where bonding between father and son is inadequate, whether through deficiencies in the father or through his absence, or both. There are a few problems with this view, in my opinion. First, many HS subjects strongly deny this set of circumstances, my own son included. Second, millions of families where such circumstances exist fail to produce HS. Family environment, however, certainly has a lot to do with the development of HS, as the incidence of the condition in siblings who have all had the same upbringing tends to suggest.

Societal approval or pressure, combined with propaganda telling him or her that change is impossible, provides a powerful set of circumstances turning confused or lonely or unhappy young people into a life of HS activity.

We have been talking about "homosexuality" as if it was a cut-and-dried condition. Actually, as in alcoholism, there are many varieties and degrees of HS, some of which are clearly temporary; e.g., HS relationships onboard ship or in prison.

The similarities between HS and alcoholism are significant, particularly in males.

Both involve a decreased chance of establishing a good marriage.

Both involve a decrease in life expectancy.

Both are associated with a list of severe or fatal diseases.

Both are associated with serious mental disease, including suicide.

Both show a low likelihood that the effects will be eliminated unless the underlying condition is changed.

Change is only seen in those who desperately want it, and success rate is thirty to fifty percent in both conditions.

Both show characteristics of addictive states; e.g., change being more easily effected in the early stages and the condition being reinforced or maintained by repeated "self-soothing" acts.

Both conditions arise from a combination of influences, some of which are not yet understood, but which include factors which are genetic, environmental, familial, circumstantial, etc., and have to do also with personality, upbringing and personal choice.

With regard to intolerance, the unforgivable sin. Tolerance is required by both parties—not coercion, threats and changes in the law. There are plenty of intolerance horror stories on both sides of the debate.

A visit to the computer of a university library will turn up many thousands of references to HS. The difficulty in finding a consensus of opinion is compounded by the fact that reputable scientific inquiry is reported in technical journals or in the depths of the Internet, but are not commonly read by the media. Furthermore, tentative scientific conclusions are jumped on by reporters who are driven by the compulsion to make it snappy, brief, politically correct, newsworthy and ahead of the competition. With complex problems which have moral, ethical, religious and sociological overtones, what chance does truth have to emerge, and what does it matter if it does or not in a postmodern world?

In 1993, Alper and Beckwith wrote in "Genetic Fatalism and Social Policy," *Yale Journal of Biology and Medicine*:

> *...whether or not a trait is genetic has little relevance to questions concerning determinism, free will and individual responsibility for actions.*

Whatever that means, it is time for a Christian to see what the Bible has to say, trying to "*speak the truth in love*," Ephesians 4:15, and remembering that "*hatred stirs up dissension*" (and dissension hatred), "*but love covers over all wrongs*" (Proverbs 10:12).

Scriptural teaching is very much more than a few proof texts. It teaches:

(a) Humanity is dimorphous, i.e., of two kinds, each complementary to the other. Their union in marriage produces a kind of completion, a state of becoming "one flesh."

(b) Each one of these two kinds is of infinite value in themselves. This value in God's eyes is independent of becoming "one flesh" with the opposite sex.

(c) In the O.T., this union is used as an illustration of the oneness of the LORD with His people—Isaiah 54:5,6... 62:4,5. Israel's unfaithfulness to the LORD was likened to adultery; see Ezekiel ch. 16 and many other references, especially the message of Hosea.

(d) In the N.T., similarly, the marriage union is likened to Christ's love for His church: Ephesians 5:23... Revelation 21:9,10... 2 Corinthians 11:2. Christ affirmed the O.T. order; Matthew 19:6... Mark 10:1–10, as did Paul also in Ephesians 5:31.

Positive teaching about sexuality, of course, has its negative side, too. Fornication, idolatry, incest, bestiality, adultery and homosexuality are all forbidden in both Old and New Testaments. None of these is singled out as worse than the other; Leviticus 18:22...20:13. The N.T. is equally specific; Romans 1:22... 1 Corinthians 6:9... 1 Timothy 1:10. See also Genesis ch. 19, Judges 19:22...2 Peter 2:6–8... Jude v. 7.

Perhaps few HS spokesmen care what the Bible says, but some deny the clear scriptural message, pointing out Jesus does not specifically condemn HS (but see Mark 7:21–23). They also say,

1) O.T. references refer to homosexuality in association with idolatrous cult practices and bear no relation to modern homosexuality. If Leviticus 18:22, etc., are to be obeyed, then all the other commandments of the law should be also. (But the N.T. gives us clear guidelines about this, as it sheds light on the O.T.)

2) HS advocates list a number of so-called HS relationships in the Bible; e.g., Ruth and Naomi, Jesus and John, Paul and Timothy, the centurion and his servant, David and Jonathan. No comment is necessary.

In the Sermon on the Mount, Jesus tightened, rather than loosened, the moral and ethical demands of the law. By contrast, some HS advocates would like to see a return to Greek and Roman culture in which HS played a part which was accepted as normal.

Homosexuals in general are not persuaded by argument and are highly skeptical of the claim that we "love the sinner but hate the sin," considering it hypocritical (and, of course, "homophobic'). Yet, watching a beloved son die of AIDS, we know from experience that it is not only possible, it is extremely easy—in fact, impossible not to do so.

I have quoted extensively from the books by Satinover and Schmidt already mentioned. They are invaluable for the Christian seeking information about homosexuality.

In spite of accusations that seem to treat *all* material critical of homosexuality as hate-inspired, the reader will find nothing in these books inciting hostility to gays. However, because of this insistence that fear and hatred are behind everything that is not supportive of the homosexual position, Christians particularly should lean over backwards to have clear consciences where their attitude to HS friends is concerned. Here is a situation where loving one's "enemies" is a test of our love and obedience to Christ Himself.

A Rare Case

Adapted from Physician, July-Aug. 2002.

IN a strange rite of hari-kari, Christian pollsters take delight—one could almost say, lick their chops—over news that, if true, gives the Christian cause bad publicity. The key words are "if true."

One example of this is the apparent relish with which they proclaim there is no difference nowadays in the incidence of marriage break-up between churchgoers and others. My immediate reaction, after mentally checking out the eighty or ninety churchgoers on our Christmas letter list, is "Hogwash!" The list comes up with a figure of about five percent. Allowing for errors and omissions, let's say ten percent—i.e., about a fifth of the current figure for all marriages in Canada. Of course, these figures confirm that many of our non-churchgoing friends have long, happy marriages, too, and thank God for that; but how can the pollsters' dismal statistics be explained?

Perhaps the answer is there were a lot of very "nominal" churchgoers who answered the inquiry questionnaire. After all, the term "churchgoer" covers a multitude of sinners. The terms "churchgoer" and "Christian" are hardly synonymous. Or perhaps there is a happier explanation. Maybe a flood of new Christians, bringing with them the baggage of their pre-churchgoing lives, have skewed the figures by their sheer numbers. I think this is a true picture of many evangelical churches, if our own church is a fair sample. May it be so!

Whatever the explanation, the case history of a very long and happy marriage may be of interest as a rare specimen. It may help set the record straight and provide encouragement to those "churchgoers" who are still determined to keep the "lock" in "wedlock." The case has been written up according to the form that was drummed into me as a medical student those many, many years ago.

The Case

A WASP couple, both born in London, England, during World War I. The husband (H) graduated in medicine from the University of London in 1940. The wife (W) did a course in pharmacy about the same time. They got engaged during the Battle of Britain in 1940 and were married four months later in an air raid. Sixty-two years later, the honeymoon is still in progress.

Family History

Both subjects came from homes with long, stable marriages. H had three brothers; one died in WWII, one died after fifty-three years of happy marriage, and one has been happily married for fifty-five years. W's only brother is also happily married after fifty-five years. Both of the couple's two surviving sons are happily married after thirty-seven and twenty-four years respectively.

Etiology

Both subjects are active Christians. Both are in good health, in their mid-eighties, though both have had life-threatening conditions in the past. (Cancer of the uterus and aortic aneurysm repair.) Economically, though things were tight during nineteen years of medical missionary life, finances are adequate in retirement.

H and W had three sons. One died in 1992, one is a dentist and one a teacher. There are seven grandchildren and four great-grandsons.

Symptoms and Signs

Both subjects hate being away from each other for more than a few hours at a time. They frequently find themselves thinking about the same thing. They share their hopes, fears, failures, successes and money, and they laugh at themselves, each other and others a lot. They survived a harrowing separation of twenty-three months, eleven hours and fourteen minutes just seven months after getting married (as did millions of others during WWII).

There have been, of course, many tense moments (as when H tipped W into the Pacific Ocean in a sailboat two minutes after assuring her such a calamity could never happen under his care). They have shared, too, the wonders of mountains in Canada and of game parks in Africa.

They shared the workload and stresses of life in one of the poorest countries in the world, and W stretched her pharmaceutical training to include nurse, anesthetist and surgical assistant on occasions, meanwhile rearing three children in the tropics. Both learned two local dialects in West Africa and survived two elections and two revolutions ("Baby Doc" Duvalier in Haiti and Field Marshal Idi Amin Dada in Uganda). Both like the music, particularly piano, of Beethoven, Bach and other classical composers. Both can tire fairly quickly of Mozart, incurring thereby the scorn of some of their friends!

H and W have shared adventures, dangers, great grief, friendships, joys and disappointments. They share a strong physical attraction for each other. They have a similar sense of humour and have done numerous skits together at camp concerts, etc. (And even a wedding or two!) More importantly, they have both, from the beginning, looked on marriage as a one-way street with NO EXIT.

Functional Inquiry

There are many incompatibilities in this couple's lives and a counsellor would probably have advised them not to get married. H is impulsive and untidy. W is cautious and neat. H sometimes feels slowed down by W, who often feels hurried by H. H loves camping and dinghy sailing, while W hates both. W loves flowers while H is only interested in edible vegetation. H likes the house fairly cool while W likes the thermostat pushed off the register. When driving, H likes the window open and W doesn't, period. H is not really interested in the Royal Family, while W is a frustrated British Empire Loyalist at heart. And on and on.

Chief Complaint

None.

Discussion

In all marriages, influencing factors may be extrinsic or intrinsic, i.e., from without or from within. Extrinsic factors include circumstances of upbringing, race, culture, health, financial stress, living conditions, etc. Of course, materialists, believing that irrational forces drive *all* events in life (with the exception of their own opinions), have no alternative but to attribute a happy marriage to these impersonal "chance" circumstances. In other words, H and W were just plain lucky.

Intrinsic factors include personal aims and ideals, world view and choices. This marriage from the beginning acknowledged Jesus as Lord, and however imperfectly that ideal was obeyed, the Saviour gradually claimed more and more territory as the years went by. H and W have no doubt that *every* influence affecting their marriage and every experience in it was directed by the Lord to whom they belonged, through no merit of their own. A Christian world view makes no distinction between extrinsic and intrinsic factors. Why, then, do Christian marriages sometimes fail?

Prognosis and Treatment

Perhaps this case study provides some clues why marriages break down.

(a) Many couples, even Christian ones, keep divorce as a sort of emergency parachute.

(b) Many do not really share their finances.

(c) Many do not pray together regularly or at all.

(d) Persistent pressure from our culture to seek one's own fulfillment first (instead of that of one's spouse) is hard to resist.

(e) Absolute honesty and openness *from the beginning* is perhaps rare.

(f) Repentance and the confession of guilt are out of style.

(g) Almost the entire world of art, literature and media opinion is against the concept of lifelong marriage.

(h) The struggle to keep up with the Joneses wrecks many marriages. Heavy debt and loaded credit cards, latchkey kids and chronic anxiety leave no time for intimacy, devotions together or parenting.

H and W consider factor (h) probably the most destructive in marriage. Affluence is more dangerous than poverty.

Conclusion

Canadian geese do not have a monopoly on mating for life. Christian marriage, like old age, is not for the faint-hearted, but it can be started, repaired and maintained for a lifetime, and its rewards are out of this world.

A Compulsory Subject

From an award-winning article for
Inscribe Christian Writers' Fellowship.

"Celebrate"—a word that seems naked without a following exclamation mark or two. Celebrate!! That's better. This was the command given to the Children of Israel on numerous occasions during their disreputable history. Set by the LORD as a required exercise, not an "optional subject" for the Chosen People, it was as though the Israelites had occasionally to be shaken out of their melancholy, their fear of enemies, their quarreling and their spiritual adultery.

So it was that God, who had chosen them above other nations, from time to time took His megaphone and shouted to them, "Celebrate! Rejoice! Let your hair down! Have a party. I am the LORD that brought you out of bondage with a mighty hand and a stretched out arm. Get with it! CELEBRATE!"

In obedience, the Israelites celebrated the Passover, the days of unleavened bread, the early harvest, the late harvest, the giving of the law, the journey through the desert, the rediscovery of the law, the narrow escape from annihilation at the time of Esther, the rebuilding of the walls of Jerusalem, the building and rebuilding of the Temple, and many other occasions public and private.

Today, as the New Israel, we have more to celebrate than Israel under the Old Covenant. They had the Word of God, given through Moses, written on tablets of stone, and His presence with them evidenced by miracles and the pillars of fire and smoke. But we have the Incarnate Word of God, evidenced by the miracle of the resurrection of Jesus from the dead, and His presence in our hearts and minds in the Person of the Holy Spirit.

Most of our Christian celebrations exalt the fulfillment of the occasions celebrated in the Old Testament. Thus we have the Lord's Supper fulfilling the Passover, Christmas celebrating the coming into the world of the One who replaced the Law by Grace (as our means of salvation), and Easter celebrating the victory of the Messiah over death.

Traditionally the Feast of Pentecost celebrated not only the harvest, but also the giving of the law on Mt. Sinai. This event was followed by rebellion and the death of three thousand people. Our own Pentecost celebrates the day the Spirit was sent to act out God's law in our hearts; fittingly, a day when three thousand people found eternal life.

Every June we celebrate our engagement, because it nourishes and revives memory, though an engagement anniversary party is not really needed to make us remember again those sunny hours on Leith Hill in Surrey, England, with the evacuation of Dunkirk filling the news. I remember, too, my utter amazement when a brown-haired young lady, smelling vaguely of ung. methyl sal. (from the dispensary where she worked) and "Tosca" (from a bottle she had applied), said, "Yes, I love you, too." Our little island was bracing for invasion by the Nazis. I could have taken them on single-handed that day!

I remember also celebrating the birthday of the Word made Flesh at Christmas in London as a child. Santa Claus (Father Christmas) was scarcely mentioned, and if he had reindeer, they were anonymous. I think my parents would have been ill at ease if they had thought we really believed in the old gentleman! We made our own "paper chains" as decorations and went to church on Christmas mornings. Christmas dinner always included a pudding I didn't particularly like but condescended to eat, as it was loaded with sixpences. I do not know how I survived those years without an emergency tracheostomy.

On Boxing Day, there was a traditional football game (soccer of course), when my father's Bible class took on all comers.

My parents, though Church of England, were staunch evangelicals, celebrating the birth of Christ with no frills attached. I vividly remember my mother's horror when her "high church" sister sent her a plaster image of the infant Christ as an aid to adoration. I can still hear her agonized cry of disgust when she opened the parcel—"Help! Florence has sent me an idol! What an *awful* thing to do!"

Later, with our young family in West Africa, our ingenuity was stretched as we made a Christmas tree out of palm branches, and toys out of scrap wood and empty powdered-milk tins, but the central emphasis was the same. We were celebrating with joy the birthday of our King.

During the last few difficult years in Sierra Leone at Christmas time, children would start coming up to the house around the end of November, singing "carols" they had made up in "English" (West African Krio). A popular one celebrated the fact that they had survived another year. "Happy Christmas, mi no die-oh, Tell God tanki fo mi life-oh!" Today, many of these same kids have been starved to death or mutilated in a country that was too busy fighting for diamond wealth and political power to celebrate the joy of Christmas. We entertained one such mutilated refugee and his family in our home during Christmas 2002.

We celebrate not only the Living Word coming into the world, but also the written Word going out into the world, translated into the languages of readers who are often hungrier than Canadians to hear it. In this, too, the memories of an old man are very vivid (see Chapter 16).

When we were in Haiti, a revolution, famine, civil unrest, and epidemics of meningitis and typhoid could not stop the celebrations when the new Haitian Creole Bibles arrived at our hospital.

For the Bible translator, there are two priceless fringe benefits. First, after a month or two, one begins to think, dream, argue and talk to oneself in the language concerned. This sort of opportunity is hard to come by today, as people in other cultures—in Africa at least—increasingly want to learn English rather than help you learn their mother tongue.

Second, dissecting each verse again and again, questioning the meaning, translating it and then proofreading it five or six times is a total immersion course in the words and teaching of Scripture. There is no better way to know and celebrate the Word than to turn it into another language.

What a joy it is to have the Word of God to celebrate. Physical life on bread alone leads to protein-calorie malnutrition, with its emaciation, pot-belly, "flakey-paint" rash, cottony ginger hair, edema and whining misery. We had a ward full of such kwashiorkor kids in Uganda. Similarly in the political realm, we all know what a culture is like that celebrates the words of humans to the exclusion of the Word of God; a culture that is fragile, fearful, complaining and swollen with luxury in places, while wasting away in others.

So we celebrate the words of humans with caution and misgiving, and the Word of God with joy and enthusiasm. The

Haitians, who sing slowly and mournfully in French, give tongue with great gusto in Haitian Creole. A popular and cynical Haitian song, paraphrased from Haitian Creole, celebrates the emptiness of human word—

> *The world is very wicked, and Satan works overtime,*
> *So you'd better watch out!*
> *If you put your trust in mankind, you'll be disappointed!*

This little bit of world-weary wisdom reflects the words of the Lord in Jeremiah 17:5. Taken by itself, it is like a diagnosis of AIDS—no cure is offered. But the Word of the Lord to Jeremiah didn't stop at verse five. We celebrate the Living Word, who provides the remedy in verse seven: *Blessed is the man who trusts in the LORD, whose confidence is in Him* (NIV).